Living Faith Journal

RESURRECTED Faith

Daily Inspirations To Obey God's WORD

D. Greg Ebie

All communication may be sent to:
Firm Foundation
D. Greg Ebie
9815 Nichols Rd.
Windham, OH 44288
greg@firmfoundationtoday.com

Firm Foundation Publishing
ISBN-13: 978-1-7364959-1-9

Contents

Living Faith Journal

This is your book and not mine. Fill its pages with your words. Allow the words of scripture to make an impression upon your mind—listen to the still small voice of the Holy Spirit speaking directly to you. As your words fill this book you will be renewed with a living faith.

In the pages that follow, you will gain a view into my journal and personal time spent with Jesus. These are shared as an example to help you learn how to discern what God is saying to you. While your experience is unique, you may from time-to-time also identify with the WORD shared because the things we face are all *"common to man"* (1 Cor. 10:13).

The WORD of God comes to us in a variety of ways, but the focus of the Living Faith Journal is for you to reflect and write the words God brings to life when you read the Bible. The scriptures are "crucially important to our everyday lives. And don't think obscure religious knowledge here. Think food. Think water. Think air." God's WORD is essential for our faith to come alive.

Your personal devotional time should not be just another box to check off a daily to-do list in an attempt to feel good about yourself. A regular quiet time to read God's WORD is how you grow in our relationship with Jesus. God wants to make Himself known to you more than you want to know Him. The words you write will ignite a greater passion for Jesus within you. Through God's WORD, the Holy Spirit will strengthen you with resurrected faith to live in obedience to what the LORD says to you.

Be an engaged and active listener. The importance of not casually listening to God's WORD cannot be understated. Too many Christians ignore what God is saying. They don't have a living faith—their faith is dead because they don't hear and obey. Your Living Faith Journal will help you in two important ways.

First, God's WORD spoken to you is timely. The LORD speaks to you in this now moment of your life. God's WORD is not like all the other words and endless chatter that try to captivate your attention each day. So much of what you hear and read are meaningless words, but

God's WORD is "living and active" to speak to you in this now moment (Heb. 4:12).

Jesus knows exactly where you are and what you need. God's WORD will speak to you about the decisions you face, the despair that leaves you in the dark, the distress and fear that seeks to paralyze you, the difficulties that overwhelm you, and the doubt that clouds your thoughts. But that's not all. God will also talk with you about the depravity of your sin and the distortion of guilt—both are chains to hold you captive and separate you from His love.

God is ready and wants to talk with you about the issues you face if only you are willing to stop and listen. Above all the noise, you need to hear God's WORD for this now moment in your life.

Second, through the Living Faith Journal, the Holy Spirit will bring God's WORD to life within you to actually live it. Don't let yourself be a passive listener. You are only fooling yourself when you don't do what God's WORD says—you're like the man who looks at himself in the mirror but forgets what he looks like the moment he walks away. You will be blessed as an active listener who is not a "hearer who forgets but a doer who acts" (Jam. 1:25). Fill the pages of this book with all that God says to you in His WORD so you can actually live it and not forget it.

The Holy Spirit will speak to us through God's WORD in this now moment to empower us to apply it in our daily lives. That's why each daily devotion in the Living Faith Journal is based upon an easy-to-remember acrostic: **W-O-R-D**.

WHISPER OF GOD

Read the scriptures slowly with a listening heart because the Holy Spirit will speak to you. Even if it is the same as what I chose, write out the verse(s) that spoke to you from the scripture reading of God's WORD.

OBSERVATION

Look at the context around what you wrote down. Ask some questions to do a little investigation. Are words repeated? Who is the audience and who is speaking? What stands out to you? Use a commentary or Bible dictionary to help you dig a little deeper. How did those who first heard this WORD from God understand it?

Insightful observation skills reveal what the scriptures mean, and not what we think or want it to mean.

REAL LIFE APPLICATION

This step is the key to obedience—to listen and obey. By making observations you put yourself into the shoes of those who first heard God's WORD so that you can properly understand it. Your response is to carry the principles taught in scripture home, to bring it from their time in history into your life today. How does God want you to respond to what you hear in your day-to-day life? Real life application means you will live differently. Write down the one thing the LORD wants you to do to apply His WORD today.

DAILY PRAYER

Finish with a two-part prayer. Begin by saying "Yes" and agree with God about what He has said. Often this involves confessing your sin of disobedience. The second step is to say, "LORD help me." You can't do what God says in your own strength—human effort seeks to force obedience through legalism. Instead, you only need to yield to the Holy Spirit who will empower you to obey God's WORD. Ask God to help you not to give in to the desires of the flesh that lead to sin, but to instead submit yourself to the Spirit, so you can live in righteousness. Make this your daily prayer to walk like Jesus according to the counsel of God's WORD.

After you write your devotional thoughts, try to include a title that summarizes what you wrote about what God said to you that day.

You are about to begin a journey that will change how you read the Bible. With resurrected faith, God's WORD will come to life in you. No longer will you think of it as dull or boring, a chore to cross off your daily to-do list. Instead, reading the scriptures will be a delight because it is time spent with the living God who speaks to you.

Another way the Holy Spirit speaks to us is through the preaching of God's WORD. As an attentive listener, you can also use the W-O-R-D devotional outline in your sermon notes. The goal is to have a living faith that listens and obeys what God says in whatever way you hear his voice—through the scriptures, a sermon, a song, whatever.

A resurrected faith awaits to empowers you to live your life in obedience to God's WORD.

The Timeless Fight for the Faith

Read Jude 1

Whisper of God

Beloved, although I was very eager to write to you
about our common salvation, I found it necessary to
write appealing to you to contend for the faith that
was once for all delivered to the saints.

Jude 1:3

Observation

Jude wanted to write about our *"common salvation."* I can only imagine what Jude's gospel story might have been like. As a half-brother to Jesus, Jude knew Jesus like Mathew, Mark, Luke, and John did not. As much as I might like to hear it, the world will never know Jude's story about the life, death, and resurrection of Jesus.

Instead, Jude had something of greater importance to write about. The gospel story about Jesus was being shared. Jude *"found it necessary to write"* about something else. His appeal is urgent, a singular heart's cry that compelled him to communicate a message of timeless importance.

Jude urged his readers to *"contend for the faith."* The KJV adds color to its translation of the Greek word **epagōnizomai**—we are to "earnestly contend."[1] The struggle for the faith is intense. Notice within the Greek word we can see the root of the English word "agony." Jude's plea was not to contemplate faith in the privacy of our quiet time. He calls for believers to join the battle and engage in a fight for the faith.

The faith for which we are to contend is far more than a trusting or believing faith. Yes, if we are honest, we all struggle from time to time with doubts of one size or another. Jude is not urging us to just believe with all our hearts. *"To contend for the faith"* means something else.

The faith we struggle for is what *"was once for all delivered to the saints."* The faith is the gospel and knowledge of who Jesus is.

1

Faith can also be used to describe the doctrine or teaching of the church. However, we must be careful that we do not just contend for a creed. We struggle to know Jesus, so our *"faith might not rest in the wisdom of men but in the power of God"* (1 Cor. 2:5). Knowing Jesus comes first, otherwise, our doctrines describe Jesus' identity according to the limitations of our God-sized boxes. Instead, we should allow the infinite reality of who God is in the person of Jesus to define our doctrine.

Real Life Application

God calls us *"to contend for the faith that was once for all delivered to the saints."* I need to join in the timeless fight for the faith and know Jesus as He is. This is the tension to comprehend the faith revealed at creation and perfectly fulfilled by Jesus. Contending for the faith is a heartfelt desire to know Jesus. After all, I'm not in love with doctrines and creeds—I want to know and love Jesus more.

Daily Prayer

LORD Jesus, I confess how I have not daily joined in the timeless fight for the faith. All too often, I'm content to go through the routine of life, rather than pressing into Your presence to know You more. Forgive me. Thank You that Your desire to make Yourself known is greater than mine to know You. You're always taking the initiative. Holy Spirit, help me to respond with a greater passion to know Christ and join in the struggle for the faith. For me to contend won't be easy—at times I will feel the agony of an age-old battle. My flesh will long for the comfort of routine, to continue walking a familiar path. Strengthen my spirit to follow where You will lead me—whether early in the morning or to break away from evening entertainment. LORD, I want to struggle to know You.

---

[1] *epagōnizomai* – Strong's Definitions. https://www.blueletterbible.org/lang/lexicon/lexicon.cfm?Strongs=G1864&t=ESV

Whisper of God

Observation

Real Life Application

Daily Prayer

Just Have Faith

Read James 2

Whisper of God

So also faith by itself, if it does not have works, is dead.

James 2:17

Observation

"Just have faith." Well-meaning Christians say these words all the time to encourage one another when going through a difficulty or hardship. I know what they mean by these three words because I have said them myself. The idea to "just have faith" is an encouragement to not give up or lose hope because we know God is working to bring us through whatever adversity we might face.

I don't think James would agree with our words of good courage. To "just have faith" is useless because *"faith by itself, if it does not have works, is dead."* James wants us to understand faith is far more than what we believe or hope for. Dead faith points only to what a person believes, while living faith includes the evidence of the works it accomplished. With resurrected faith, what we believe activates and directs what we do.

In English, we have no concept of faith as a verb that is active. We understand faith as a noun—something that you either have or do not. Greek thinking is different because the noun "faith" comes from the word "faith" as a verb. Genuine faith is active and works within us.

We need a paradigm shift to understand faith as a verb. Faith does something deep within us. In Christ "faithing" shapes and transforms the person we are—how we think, what we say, and the things we do.

Faith is more than an attitude of hope or just trusting in God to do something for us. Faith is active within us—"faithing" believes God empowers us to act and do what we are otherwise powerless to do on our own.

I remember times when I faced the so-called unexpected storms of life. I felt impotent because I was powerless to do anything about my situation. "Faithing" will cause the lifeless noun of faith to come alive within me, to become a verb of activity, and change me from the inside out.

The work of faith in difficult times might be to get up and face the day with a positive attitude, to stop sharing my complaints, and express thanks instead. Faith as a verb will open my hand to share without expecting anything in return—to freely give rather than feel like I never have enough. "Faithing" will motivate my feet and hands to do what is needed, rather than hope others step in with a handout.

Real Life Application

I need to think about faith differently and understand it as a verb, so my dead faith comes alive through the activity of "faithing."

Daily Prayer

LORD Jesus, I confess my faith is sometimes dead so that I do what is contrary to what my faith believes. Forgive me. Holy Spirit, resurrect my faith so it is alive within me. Thank You that this is not a work I have to try to do—human energy is far too weak. Your Spirit lives within me and provides the spark that brings my faith alive. Help me comprehend how faith is more than something I possess or give intellectual agreement to. "Faithing" is the activity of faith to transform me into the person you created me to be. "Faithing" will energize my life to live what I say I believe.

Whisper of God

Observation

Real Life Application

Daily Prayer

Naughty or Nice?

Whisper of God

For by grace you have been saved through faith. And this is not your own doing; it is the gift of God, not a result of works, so that no one may boast.

Ephesians 2:8-9

Observation

The kid in me remembers reading this letter to Santa. "Dear Santa, let me explain! See what happened was…well see it went like this…uh, one day I was…, uh, dang, I'm getting coal huh?" Once upon a Christmas, I feared being on the NAUGHTY list but wanted so badly to be on the NICE list.

I've come to realize that sometimes we treat Jesus just like Santa. We think we need to do something to earn our salvation and forget, that just like the presents under the Christmas tree, salvation is a gift.

To try to earn salvation and tip the heavenly scales of justice in our favor with more good deeds than bad is impossible. We're powerless to do anything to change our fate because we *"were dead in the trespasses and sins"* (Eph. 2:1). The dead can do nothing for themselves.

We are saved *"through faith"* and nothing else. We want to make up for what we did, to try to earn God's grace, but salvation is not our own doing, *"it is the gift of God, not a result of works."*

Even faith is not something we do, but the moment we believe the activity of "faithing" does its work in us, so we are no longer dead, but are made alive in Christ. Paul described this activity of faith in the Ephesians as the power of God that *"worked in Christ when He raised Him from the dead"* (Eph.1:20).

After Jesus died on the cross, He was laid cold and lifeless in the grave and was powerless to raise Himself from the dead. But the miracle worker who raised others from the dead believed the Holy Spirit would breathe life into His dead body. On the third day, dead

Jesus could still do nothing, until through faith His life was restored, and the victorious living Jesus came out of the tomb.

No need to write Jesus a letter, or to try to explain—He already knows we're dead in our sin and unable to do anything about it. But the moment we have faith to believe, His life floods into ours so that we become *"His workmanship, created in Christ Jesus for good works"* (Eph. 2:10).

We've got it backward. As much as we want to do good works to earn our salvation, we can't. "Faithing" brings us into salvation bringing us from death to life. Faith animates our body, soul, and spirit to live differently and do the good Jesus intended all along.

Real Life Application

We don't often think of Jesus having faith, or that His faith was active within Him. But Jesus is the author of our faith. What He believed was "faithing" within Him so that Jesus not only knew the Holy Spirit would breathe life into His dead body, but our Savior also knew the Spirit would breathe life into all who believe. The faith of Jesus worked in Him so that with joy He *"endured the cross"* knowing all that was to come (Heb. 12:2).

The kid in me still sometimes tries to get off the NAUGHTY list. I need to remember I'm powerless to change my life—salvation is a gift through faith. And by that same faith working within me, I can live victoriously just like Jesus. My human effort will never be enough, but "faithing" enables me to do the NICE things God created me for.

Daily Prayer

LORD Jesus, thank You for the gift of salvation. I know your forgiveness and love are impossible to earn. Forgive me when I still try in my own strength to deserve Your gift. My effort causes me to grow weary and lose the joy of Your salvation. Holy Spirit, help me always have childlike faith and allow "faithing" to bring what I believe to life in what I think, say, and do. Jesus, help me follow Your example. You did not try to earn the Father's approval, but through faith suffered, died, and was raised, so that now You are *"seated at the right hand of the throne of God"* (Heb. 12:2).

Whisper of God

Observation

Real Life Application

Daily Prayer

12

An Example of Faith at Work in Ordinary People

Read 1 Thessalonians 1

Whisper of God

We give thanks to God always for all of you, constantly mentioning you in our prayers, remembering before our God and Father your work of faith and labor of love and steadfastness of hope in our LORD Jesus Christ.

1 Thessalonians 1:2-3

Observation

One thing we never wanted our children to say was, "I can't." A willingness to try and fail is far better than quitting and throwing in the proverbial towel often before even trying. Unfortunately, my kids are not the only ones who wanted to give up. I've been guilty of telling God, "I can't."

When someone thinks they can't do something, an attempt to force them is useless. Their mind is made up. Regardless of how big or small a task might be, they believe they can't do it.

What people need is an example to follow. A simple instruction to show how something is done with an illustration or two of how others have done it is powerful.

The believers in the church at Thessalonica provide us an example of how faith does its work in and through ordinary people. These were not super saints, but people just like us. When they heard the gospel, they were saved by their faith in Christ. What they believed began the work of "faithing" to produce their *"work of faith and labor of love and steadfastness of hope."*

Paul said the *"work of faith"* enabled these first century believers to *"become imitators of us and of the LORD"* (v. 6). And let's not make the mistake of thinking they had it easy because they came to faith *"in much affliction"* (v. 6). Their decision to be a Christian meant facing adversity—unlike the choice many of us make today, theirs was a difficult path to follow.

Their faith not only enabled them to follow the examples set before them in the way they lived, but they also *"became an example to all the believers"* (v. 7). The good report about these people spread everywhere because the work of faith strengthened them to turn *"to God from idols to serve the living and true God"* (v. 9). And theirs was a faith that endured and did not give up as they waited in hope *"for [God's] Son from heaven"* (v. 10).

Real Life Application

I can't help but think of how I often taught both my children and adults how to do things. I showed them how to do it, watched them do it, and encouraged them to continue to do it.

We see the work of faith impacting the lives of ordinary people in much the same way. Jesus leads the way as an example for others to follow. Paul followed Christ's example, but he didn't keep his faith to himself. The believers in Thessalonica followed both Paul's and the LORD'S example. Paul also encouraged others, like the Corinthians to do the same. (See 1 Cor. 11:1).

The work of faith in us should not be a personal or private matter. Instead, we need the work of faith God is doing in us to be on display for others to see so they can learn to follow our example.

I need to seek out a trusted friend who can be my example and encourage me to be faithful to the work of faith in me. And, in turn, I also need to set the example of faith for others, both Christian and non-Christian, so they can see how God can help them to let the work of faith be effective in them.

Daily Prayer

LORD Jesus, I confess that I have sometimes been guilty of believing the lie that says I can't. Yet regardless of what You may ask me to do, You have asked other believers to do the same and they did it. Just like the Thessalonian church, ordinary people just like me are allowing the work of faith to be done in them. Forgive me for the times when I said, "I can't" and given in to my fear or just wanted to remain comfortable and not step out in obedience. Holy Spirit, help me to have a trusted friend I can be honest with and who can be an example for me to follow. And LORD, give me a willing heart to be that kind of friend for someone else, so they can see in me how the work of faith transformed this ordinary guy into the person you created me to be.

Whisper of God

Observation

Real Life Application

Daily Prayer

The Absolute Assurance of Faith

Read Hebrews 10

Whisper of God

*Let us draw near with a true heart in full assurance of faith,
with our hearts sprinkled clean from an evil conscience and
our bodies washed with pure water*

Hebrews 10:39

Observation

Faith is not a fantasy. Our foundation is not an empty hope. Our faith is a complete certainty. We have an unshakeable bedrock of faith upon which to build our lives. Rather than being based upon anything we do for ourselves, our faith is grounded in Christ Jesus.

The faith of the ancients was weak in comparison to what ours can be. They had to come each year to offer sacrifices. What they did in obedience to God's instruction was only *"a shadow of the good things to come"* and *"a reminder of sins every year"* (vv. 1, 3).

The strength of our faith to cleanse us from sin is not found in the sacrifice of animals. Instead, we are *"sanctified though the offering of the body of Jesus Christ once for all"* (v. 10). The work Jesus did at the cross is finished, so He is seated *"at the right hand of God"* (v. 12).

How is our faith been strengthened by what Jesus did for us? The ancients believed and followed God's instructions, but the law was external being written on tablets of stone and scrolls. Now because of what Jesus accomplished on our behalf, the Holy Spirit fulfills the LORD's promise to *"put my laws on their hearts and write them on their minds"* (v. 16).

God's covenant is no longer separate from us but is within our hearts—it's no longer external but internal. Our faith is grounded upon the same law as the ancients but is strengthened because the location of God's instructions is now written upon our hearts.

As a result, our faith should be stronger than the ancients. They relied upon a priest to bring their offering before God, but we *"have confidence to enter the holy places by the blood of Jesus"* (v. 19). We can draw near to God not through anything we did, but with an unwavering faith in what Jesus did for us.

In turn, the Spirit energizes what is written upon our hearts, and the work of "faithing" enables us to live what we believe as an example *"to stir up one another to love and good works, not neglecting to meet together"* (v. 24-25). With an absolute assurance of faith, we are not like *"those who shrink back and are destroyed"* through disobedience, but with faithful obedience *"preserve [our] souls"* (v. 39).

Real Life Application

When we cut away the chapter division, Hebrews 11 follows verse 39 with examples of how the ancients lived by faith, so let's not believe the lie that we could never have such a strong faith. The enemy uses guilt to keep us bound to our sin, so we don't live with unshakable faith.

I need to allow the absolute assurance of faith to do its work in me because my heart is *"sprinkled clean from and evil conscience, and [my body is] washed with pure water"* (v. 22). This means I must look two places to strengthen my faith—to the cross in thanksgiving and prayer where Jesus did the work, and to the scriptures that illuminate the covenant written upon my heart.

Daily Prayer

LORD Jesus, I confess that I have allowed myself to think I could not be a man of faith like Abraham or Paul. I let the enemy paralyze me with guilt to keep me from being the person you created me to be. Forgive me for my weak faith. Holy Spirit, do the work of "faithing" in me so I will have an absolute assurance of faith. Turn my eyes to the cross. Thank You, LORD, that You did for me what I could not accomplish even with the sacrifice of animals—You have once and for all set me free from my sin. And continue to awaken me to Your word, which strengthens my faith and purifies me through *"the washing of the word"* (Eph. 5:26). Let this steadfast hope grow stronger in me—I praise You because Your word of the covenant is written upon my heart to give me both the desire and ability to live in obedience through faith.

Whisper of God

Observation

Real Life Application

Daily Prayer

Nothing's Better Than the Real Thing

Read Acts 17

Whisper of God

Men of Athens, I perceive that in every way you are very religious. For as I passed along and observed the objects of your worship, I found also an altar with this inscription: "To the unknown god." What therefore you worship as unknown, this I proclaim to you.

Acts 17:22-23

Observation

Paul was in Athens waiting for his friends. As he explored, he was *"provoked"* because *"the city was full of idols"* (v. 16). Paul was more than a little irritated. Every idol he saw turned up the heat within his heart. Paul burned with anger.

I find it interesting he became so infuriated because the Greek word translated *"provoked"* is used only one other time in the New Testament. Paul used it to describe how love *"is not irritable"* (1 Cor. 13:5). Paul was enraged like a husband or wife grieved and outraged by the discovery of their spouse's repeated adultery and betrayal. In the same way, Paul's love for Christ churned with anger for the countless ways the people of Athens were unfaithful to the living God.

When Paul had the opportunity to speak, he did not lash out in anger. Instead, he recognized their religious devotion and called attention to one of their many idols with the inscription *"To the unknown god."* Paul went on to proclaim Christ, the living God.

As Paul spoke, he reasoned that nothing's better than the real thing. His argument urged the men of Athens to think about three critical concerns. First, manmade idols disappoint us because the promises they make leave us empty and longing for what is always just out of reach. Jesus satisfies the deep yearning of our souls.

The second issue to consider is that carved idols covered in gold or silver deceive. An idol lies and convinces us that we are in control of our destiny. Jesus tells us the truth and shows us the way of salvation. When we believe the lie that we are in control, we also believe the lie that God is not in control.

This leads to the third problem with idols—they destroy and lead to death. An idol's promise of better tomorrows and their deception to chart our course to happiness blinds us to the coming judgment. God will not always overlook man's ignorance but has set a day to judge the world. Jesus, the righteous judge, is the only way to receive life. God proved this *"by raising Him from the dead"* (v. 31).

Real Life Application

A walk through the local grocery store isles reveals lots of generic products that claim to be as good as the real thing. Colas, chips, cookies, and more pretend to be the original, but nothing is as good as the real thing. The same is true for the idols that try to take the place of Jesus.

When Paul walked through Athens, an ancient writer states there were 30,000 idols. The population of the city in the first century was declining and may have been as low as 10,000. That's a 3 to 1 ratio, but it sounds about right for the number of idols we have in our lives today.

We may not call them gods, but we have three idols in our lives. They go by many different names, but we give ourselves to idols of control, pleasure, and wealth. Like those in Athens, we need to be awakened to the reality that nothing's better than the real thing.

I need a more intimate knowledge of who Jesus is—He is the one true and living God. In knowing Jesus, my faith will be genuine and not based on the lies of false gods.

Daily Prayer

LORD Jesus, forgive me for my idolatry. All too often I want to be in control, find pleasure, and have greater wealth. I have looked to idols for what only You can provide. I praise You as the one who keeps Your promises and satisfies my soul. Only You have authority to direct me in the way of righteousness and power to give me life eternal.

Cleanse my heart from false gods. Holy Spirit, give me a deeper love for Jesus with discernment to recognize imitation idols that want to take His place in my life. Help me to be provoked, like Paul, by any would-be god that's not the real thing.

Whisper of God

Observation

Real Life Application

Daily Prayer

Now "Faithing" in Action

Read Hebrews 11

Whisper of God

*Now faith is the assurance of things hoped for, the
conviction of things not seen … And without faith it
is impossible to please Him, for whoever would
draw near to God must believe that He exists and
that He rewards those who seek Him.*

Hebrews 11:1, 6

Observation

Hebrews 11 is often known as the "Faith Hall of Fame." We read the stories of great men and women of the faith. Abel, Enoch, Abraham, Sarah, Moses, Rahab, David, and others all lived by faith. Some unnamed heroes were even willing to be killed for their faith in God.

However, before their many stories of faith were told, the writer of Hebrews gave us a three-part definition of what faith is. First, faith is *"Now faith"* that is presently active in our lives (v. 1). Faith is not something we hold onto from the past, but it is at work today.

Secondly, *"Now faith"* is described as *"the assurance of things hoped for, the conviction of things not see"* (v. 1). We saw in the previous chapter how the confidence of our faith is grounded in what Jesus did for us. Our hope then is not to win the lottery, get a new car, or anything else we might wish for in this world. "Now faith" sees what cannot otherwise be seen and knows what is impossible to be known any other way.

Finally, "now faith" is what pleases God. The Greek word for faith is used in verse six as both a noun and a verb. *"Without faith,"* the noun, *"it is impossible to please God."* We don't make God happy because we hold to a certain doctrine. Instead, the LORD is pleased when our faith causes us to "draw near to God" because we "believe that He exists" faith as a verb. The Holy Spirit energizes the activity of "faithing," so our belief comes alive to live what we say we believe.

With a knowledge of what faith is, we can understand how it was at work to transform the lives of those listed in the "Faith Hall of

Fame." These were ordinary people who heard God's Word and allowed the work of "faithing" to enable them to live what they believed. If "now faith" was effective in their lives, then we can have now "faithing" in action in our lives today.

Real Life Application

The Holy Spirit has helped me to comprehend how faith is more than a noun of belief in doctrinal. While this is important, comatose inactive truth is useless. Faith is also a verb that makes what I believe real by how I think, speak and act.

I need to allow now "faithing" to be active in my life to transform the way I live from day-to-day making me a man of faith who pleases God.

Daily Prayer

LORD Jesus, I want to be a man who makes You happy. Forgive me for the times when I let my faith lay dormant. Your desire is for me to have "now faith" that impacts my life today. Holy Spirit, help me continue to apply the truth of scripture with "faithing" to transform how I live. Help me to live what I believe and make choices that agree with my faith.

Whisper of God

Observation

Real Life Application

Daily Prayer

Stubborn Tenacious Faith that Won't Give-up

Read Luke 18

Whisper of God

Nevertheless, when the Son of Man comes,
will He find faith on earth?

Luke 18:8

Observation

Jesus told the parable of the persistent widow to teach His disciples they should pray and not give up. I for one must admit that I don't pray nearly as much as I should. Not only do I need to apply this scripture in my life to be more prayerful, but I also need to be more persistent with the absolute assurance of faith God will hear and answer my prayer.

The question I ask myself after reading Jesus' short story is, "Okay that's great, but how do I do it?" The answer is found within Jesus' question, *"When the Son of Man comes, will He find faith on the earth?"* (v. 8).

We are living in the last days that will culminate in Jesus' Second Coming. We must take Jesus' question seriously and try to understand exactly what He means because He will be looking for faith among us.

When Jesus returns, He will NOT be looking for a generic faith among many. Translators left out a small but important word from the original Greek. Translators omitted the word *ho*. Without this word one might think Jesus will only look to find "a faith."

However, *ho* points to a specific faith as a definite article. Jesus' question would be better stated as "When I return will I find *THE* faith or *THIS/THAT kind of* faith?[1]

If we think Jesus will return looking for *"THE faith,"* then He wants to find the faith He established at creation and entrusted to the saints once and for all time. (See Jude 1:3 and "The Timeless Fight of Faith" p. 1.) If on the other, hand we take Jesus to ask if He will find *"THIS/THAT kind of faith"* when He returns, then He will be

29

searching to find a stubborn tenacious faith that won't give up like that of the persistent widow.

Real Life Application

I know from experience that my willpower and energy are not enough for me to pray more regardless of how much I know I should. To grasp the full meaning of Jesus' question, the key is to have an active resurrected faith. Both *THE* faith and *THIS/THAT kind of* faith will be found by Jesus when He returns.

I need to allow the Holy Spirit to do the work of "faithing" in me, not only so I will live what we believe, but also to energize my prayer life. Only then will Jesus find *THE/THIS* faith He is looking for in me.

Daily Prayer

LORD Jesus, forgive me for my prayerlessness. You know how I have tried and failed when I try to apply my willpower and self-discipline to the problem. In the end, I only feel guilty for not doing what I know I should, which makes me want to quit and separates me from Your presence. Holy Spirit, help me have the strength I need. Put within my heart *THE* faith Jesus gave to us and activate it with the work of "faithing" to be *THIS/THAT* kind of faith—a stubborn tenacious faith that won't give up.

---

[1] Lexicon :: Strong's G3588 - *ho* – the definite article: the, this, that. https://www.blueletterbible.org/lang/lexicon/lexicon.cfm?Strongs=G3588&t=ESV

Whisper of God

31

Observation

Real Life Application

Daily Prayer

Supersize My Faith

Read Matthew 6

Whisper of God

O you of little faith.

Matthew 6:30

Observation

Wherever we go today, things are supersized. Restaurants and retailers want me to believe bigger is better. I can get more for my money if I'm willing to up-size my order. I can get a bigger drink and more fries with my burger. My computer can have a faster processing speed and more memory. TVs can be larger with more depth of color, while smartphones offer the same resolution with more pixels in the palm of my hand.

Jesus wants me to supersize my faith. I don't want Jesus to look at me and say, *"O you of little faith."* So how can my faith be enlarged?

We could focus on the anxiety about the things that make up our lives. Worries about our stuff can consume our thinking. Jesus said the cure is to *"seek first the kingdom of God and His righteousness"* because then *"all these things will be added to you"* (v. 33). But to understand what Jesus means, we need to make some important connections in what He said.

For us to apply *"seek first the kingdom of God"* to our lives, we need to pay attention to what Jesus said right before the "Therefore." What Jesus said about everything that concerns us is connected to how many masters we serve. Jesus said we cannot *"serve God and money"* (v. 24).

The word translated money is mammon. More than dollars and cents or silver and gold, mammon refers to all the things we possess that make up our wealth. Jesus sets mammon up as a rival god that also seeks our love and devotion. At the end of the day, I have to choose whether I will love and serve the LORD or all of my stuff. The choice seems easy, that is until I read Jesus' illustration of what it looks like for mammon to take the love and devotion God deserves.

Jesus said, *"do not be anxious about your life"* about what I will eat, or the clothes I wear. But the list of things that demand my attention and causes me to worry does not end there. I will think about my house, cars, furniture, TV, cellphone, computer, lawnmower, and the list goes on and on. We have so many things that make up our lives to worry about if we let them begin to push God to the side.

The more we are anxious about the stuff that makes up our lives, our mammon, the less we love God and the smaller and less effective our faith becomes.

Real Life Application

As I think about Jesus' desire for me to supersize my faith, I can't help but think about what He said about having a mustard seed of faith. With what we consider a relatively small amount of faith Jesus said, *"you will say to this mountain, 'move from here to there,' and it will move, and **nothing will be impossible for you"*** (Matt. 17:21).

Supersizing our faith is not about the quantity or magnitude of our faith. We don't need more and more faith. Our faith is enlarged as it becomes effective in our lives. The mustard seed starts out small but grows into a large tree where birds can build their nests. This is the work of "faithing" so what I believe is energized by the Holy Spirit and I live what I believe.

I need my faith to be supersized, so I have a greater love and devotion for Jesus and have less concern for the rival god of my stuff.

Daily Prayer

LORD Jesus, forgive me for my lack of faith that causes me to put my things before You. Forgive my anxious thoughts that sometimes fill my mind. What I imagine will bring satisfaction actually sucks the life out of me—worry only makes me more tired. Holy Spirit, supersize my faith so what I believe is effective in shaping how I live my life. LORD, I want You to have the rightful place upon the throne of my heart. You alone deserve my love, my praise, my all. Enlarge my faith so I have more contentment and confidence. Contentment to be thankful and satisfied for all that I have, and confidence to know that You will provide everything I need.

Whisper of God

35

Observation

Real Life Application

Daily Prayer

The Test of Faith

Read James 1

Whisper of God

*Count it all joy, my brothers, when you meet trials
of various kinds, for you know that the testing
of your faith produces steadfastness.*

James 1:2-3

Observation

When we go through anything from a major ordeal to a minor inconvenience, we are uncomfortable and feel the anxiety and sadness that comes with trouble. Whether emotional heartache, physical trauma, or a combination of both, no one likes pain of any kind.

But James tells us we are to *"Count it all joy…when [we] meet trials of various kinds."* At first glance, I'm tempted to say, "James, you don't understand how hard life can be in the twenty-first century." The pressures of life today can seem relentless.

But then I realize James and other first century believers faced hardships, unlike anything I have ever known. They went through a famine, but my cupboards have never been empty. Worse than that, James was writing to Jewish Christians, *"the twelve tribes in the Dispersion"* (v. 1). Persecution for their faith, everything from arrests to imprisonment and execution, caused believers to flee their homes. James knew what he was talking about when it came to *"trials of various kinds."*

So whatever test life may bring our way, James tells us to *"Count it all joy."* Other translations say "consider" or "think." But I think the Greek word James used is more forceful in its meaning. The first definition is "to lead, to go before, to be a leader, to rule, command, to have authority."[1] Joy is far more than a passing thought or idea. When trials cause our thoughts to become anxious and filled with fear, when we are overcome by grief, or when our imagination runs wild, we are to take charge of how we think. When joy is the furthest thing from our minds, we are to govern our attention and fill our thoughts with joyful hope instead.

James not only encourages us to direct our thinking, he tells us the reason why. Be joyful because "you know that the testing of your faith produces steadfastness." The difficulties of life that the enemy intends for evil to weaken our faith, God will work for our good to strengthen our faith.

Whatever trial we may face activates our faith. The testing of our faith is the catalyst of "faithing" to do its work and develop perseverance.

Real Life Application

The past year had more than its share of ups and downs. Unfortunately, I did not always consider these difficulties with joy, but just endured until it was over. I can only imagine how much stronger my faith might be today if I had taken charge of my thoughts. Rather than escape my reality through a TV show or movie, I needed to direct my thoughts to joy knowing God was at work.

The LORD knows the end from the beginning—He knows the trials we will face in the days leading up to Jesus' return. Things will seem to go from bad to worse, but Jesus wants us to persevere. I need to remember to govern every painful thought and turn it into joy.

Daily Prayer

LORD Jesus, forgive me for not letting You do the work of strengthening my faith through trials. All too often I ran away from my problems to find momentary pleasure. When I want to be a couch potato and withdraw from the problems of life, remind me to be determined to take authority over my thinking. Holy Spirit, help me to see how You are at work in the trials to build steadfastness of faith. Let joy be my focus when the test of faith comes my way.

---

[1] Thayer's Greek Lexicon. (https://www.blueletterbible.org/lang/lexicon/lexicon.cfm?Strongs=G2233&t=ESV)

Whisper of God

Observation

Real Life Application

Daily Prayer

Hope within the Hardship

Read 1 Samuel 18-20; Psalm 40

Whisper of God

Be pleased, O LORD, to deliver me! O LORD,
make haste to help me…
May all who seek you rejoice and be glad in you;
may those who love your salvation say continually,
"Great is the LORD!"

Psalm 40:13, 16

Observation

David learned to trust God during the great trials test that tested his faith. Through everything he faced, David persevered and waited *"patiently for the LORD"* (Psa. 40:1).

The prophet Samuel anointed David to be Israel's king. The LORD told Samuel David was not chosen because of things man considers greatness—David was an unknown shepherd. Instead, God saw what no one else did. David had a heart of faith to pursue God.

As the anointed king, God began the work to elevate David in the eyes of Israel with great victories like the one over Goliath. But David's success only made king Saul jealous, and he grew to despise David greatly. In time, Saul saw David as the usurper of the throne and wanted to have him killed, so David had to flee for his life.

While Saul's hatred for David continued to grow, David trusted the LORD even when it was difficult. Twice things happened that king Saul was vulnerable. David's mighty men encouraged him to take Saul's life because God delivered him into his hand. But David refused to take revenge and kill Saul because as Israel's king, Saul was the LORD'S anointed.

I can imagine David's frustration. While I've never had my life threatened, I can relate to how David must have felt. I've experienced the disdain, jealousy, and even hatred of some people. I know what it feels like to want to get even when people mistreat you. However, I struggle to comprehend how David remained patient.

For David, waiting patiently with steadfast hope to trust God was a matter of life and death. This is not something you can do yourself. David's faith was active and enabled him to live what he believed with patience.

The scriptures tell us the rest of the story. In God's time, Saul was killed, and David became Israel's new king just as the LORD had promised.

Real Life Application

Unlike David, I'm not always patient. Rather than wait in hope, I'm quick to try to fix things when life gets hard to rush in, solve the problem, and save the day. I need to slow down and not be quick to act but hold on with unwavering faith in the LORD to work things out in His time and not mine.

Daily Prayer

LORD Jesus, thank you for Your faithfulness in my life. Forgive me for the times when I am too quick to act and do what I think is right rather than wait patiently for You to do what is best. Help me to slow down and look to You in prayer and trust You for the solution rather than taking matters into my own hands. You know the weight upon my heart today and the weariness I feel from day-to-day. Holy Spirit strengthen my faith. Remind me of Your promises for You are faithful. Give me a discerning ear to recognize Your voice through all of the world's noise and distractions. May I hear again of Your faithfulness and sing *"Great is the LORD!"*

Whisper of God

Observation

Real Life Application

Daily Prayer

Finding Joy within Conflict

Read 2 Corinthians 1-2

Whisper of God

*Not that we lord it over your faith, but we work with you
for your joy, for you stand firm in your faith.*

2 Corinthians 1:24

Observation

Acts 18 tells how Paul came to Corinth. As was his custom, he first preached Christ among the Jews, but they rejected his message. The LORD encouraged him to remain and over the next year and a half, Paul established a Gentile church in the city. But because of his success, the Jews in Corinth again stirred up trouble for Paul. He soon left and made his way to Ephesus.

Unfortunately, the church in Corinth fell into disarray. To deal with the conflict and sin within the church, Paul may have written as many as four letters to the church. Unresolved difficulties within the church led to Paul's *"painful visit"* and a letter he wrote *with "much affliction and anguish of heart and with many tears"* (2 Cor. 2:1, 4). Such a description does not seem to fit the tone of 1 Corinthians, and scholars debate whether or not 2 Corinthians is one letter or two. All this to say, Paul's letter to the Corinthians must be understood within the context of a dysfunctional church that struggled with infighting and disobedience.

Despite all the trouble in Corinth, Paul remained confident that they would share in the same comfort God had provided to him and his companions. As their affliction continued, Paul asked for the church to help them in prayer. Paul recognized that he was the focus of much of the conflict in Corinth. The people within the church essentially accused him of being double-minded and not being true to his word, which leads to the encouragement that *"all the promises of God find their Yes in Him"* (2 Cor. 1:20).

Paul assured the church that he did not come to them so they would not have to endure further conflict. Paul's faith was more than trusting God to help resolve the disagreement with the Corinthians. His faith was active—"faithing" enabled him to see the situation from a different perspective.

And so with strong faith, Paul would not let himself think negatively toward those who questioned his integrity. He wrote that he did not want to *"lord it over your faith,"* Instead, Paul found joy to work together because *"you stand firm in your faith"* (2 Cor. 1:24).

Real Life Application

I must labor to pray with and for those who disagree with me. We will share in God's comfort, and our prayers will enable us to stand firm in the faith.

Daily Prayer

LORD Jesus, forgive me for the times I spoke in anger and questioned the faith and love of other believers. What I considered righteous indignation did not help to maintain unity within Your Church. The enemy sowed the seeds of division and disagreement to stir up trouble among Your children. Holy Spirit, help us to not argue over disputable matters. Give me the wisdom to stand firm in the faith, a faith shared with those who sometimes disagree with me. Our faith is stronger when we focus on what we share in common. Help us to stand together so Your work of joy might be made complete in us.

Whisper of God

Observation

Real Life Application

Daily Prayer

When Doubt Brings Out Our Worst

Read Luke 7

Whisper of God

The disciples of John reported all these things to him.
And John, calling two of his disciples to him,
sent them to the LORD, saying,
"Are you the one who is to come,
or shall we look for another?"

Luke 7:18-19

Observation

Backstory time—John the Baptist was Jesus' forerunner and prepared the way. He preached a message of repentance that called people to turn from their sins because God's kingdom was near. John was not soft in his how he communicated his message but even challenged the religious leaders for their hypocrisy. The news about John spread far and wide, so lots of people came to be baptized by him in the Jordan River.

Jesus also came to be baptized by John. When he saw Jesus, John told his disciples *"Behold, the Lamb of God, who takes away the sin of the world"* (John 1:29). Later, John told them Jesus *"must increase, but I must decrease"* (John 3:30).

John the Baptist had a strong faith. He knew who he was, and he knew who Jesus was. This combination enabled him to live what he believed.

Now fast forward to Luke 7.

John the Baptist was arrested and put in prison. When some of his disciples visited him, they told him about Jesus' teaching, His miracles, and popularity among the people. Jesus had increased just like John said, and people were beginning to think that Jesus was God's anointed one, the Messiah.

Rather than being encouraged, John was overcome with doubt and questioned what he believed and said about Jesus. John sent his followers away to ask Jesus, *"Are you the one who is to come, or shall we look for another?"* (Luke 7:19).

In prison, John was at his lowest. I don't think John ever imagined things would turn out this bad. Fear and uncertainty caused him to question whether or not Jesus was the Lamb of God and the promised Messiah. Alone and locked in a cell, John's confidence that he heard God and declared the truth about Jesus was shaken. Doubt brought out his worst thoughts.

When Jesus was asked John's question, He responded with words of encouragement. Rather than chastise John for his unbelief, Jesus reassured him with the evidence of Jesus' miracles and preaching of the good news that John was right in all he said and believed. Jesus went on and told the crowd that John was more than a prophet because as His messenger there was *"none greater than John"* (Luke 7:28).

When doubt about Jesus brought out John's worst, Jesus responded with the best words of encouragement to elevate John to his rightful place as a faithful witness.

Real Life Application

When disbelief causes me to question Jesus, I need to be like John and share my doubts. Rather than focus on my circumstances, I need to listen to the word of encouragement from God, because when I'm at my worst, God's best is on the way.

Daily Prayer

LORD Jesus, I confess my doubt. You know how I sometimes question myself and You when things get difficult and the unexpected happens. I'm thankful You are not being quick to disown those overcome by uncertainty. When John was at his worst, You were at Your best for him. Jesus, You became the least in the kingdom when as an obedient servant You suffered and died in our place on the cross. You have shown us true greatness in what it means to be a servant. You remain faithful even when I'm at my worst and will encourage me to not lose heart. Help me, like John, to be steadfast in my commitment and accept my lot in life knowing the best is yet to come.

Whisper of God

Observation

Real Life Application

Daily Prayer

Don't Quit When Life Isn't Fair

Read Exodus 3-5

Whisper of God

*The LORD look on you and judge, because you
have made us stink in the sight of Pharaoh
and his servants, and have put a sword in their
hand to kill us.*

Exodus 5:21

Observation

Today I did the funeral for a saint of God who came to the end of her journey after more than 86 years. She was prepared for this day and gave me her instructions for her funeral service. She wrote out the seven things for her children to remember. Her reminders included "Life is not fair" and "Never give up." These were reminders the children of Israel needed to hear.

Moses returned to Egypt after his mountain top experience with the LORD. He and Aaron shared with the people of Israel how God would deliver them and they believed. But after Moses and Aaron appeared before Pharaoh, life went from bad to worse because the people had to make bricks without the provision straw. The taskmasters beat them because they did not make their assigned quota of bricks. Life had not treated them fairly, and the people of Israel began to complain against Moses.

The faith of Moses was being tested. He said to the LORD, *"Why did you ever send me…You have not delivered Your people at all"* (Exodus 5:22-23). Although Moses' faith was weak, he had a revelation of God as the ever-present *"I AM"* at the burning bush (Exodus 3:14). "Faithing" brought Moses' faith to life, and he chose to allow God to empower him through what he believed.

Moses spoke the LORD'S word before Pharaoh. True to His Word, the LORD did everything Moses said. Egypt was overcome, little by little, by the by plagues of judgment that worked for Israel's deliverance.

Initially, Pharaoh and the Egyptians continued to make life even harder for the people of Israel. The people continued to complain that life was not fair. Even after the LORD delivered them from Egypt, they were afraid they would die in the wilderness and wanted to return. While it took time to get Egypt out of their hearts, God was faithful to His people even when they were faithless.

The LORD'S presence and power were with them to resurrect their faith. The plagues, the crossing of the Red Sea, the destruction of Pharaoh and his chariots, the provision of manna, and so much more was God's way to teach His people "faithing"—to live what they believed and never give up.

Real Life Application

Remember this lesson: Life is not fair but never give up. Live the faith I believe because God is working His purposes even when I can't see it or understand it.

Daily Prayer

LORD Jesus, thank You for the heritage of faith and wisdom passed on by those who have served You all their lives. We all experience the unexpected in our lives. Forgive me when, like Moses and the people of Israel, I dare to question You and complain that life is not fair. Holy Spirit, help me trust You even when things in my life don't turn out as I had hoped. Empower me with a living faith that is active and never gives up. You have revealed Yourself to me in Jesus, so enable me to live what I believe and persevere according to Your unfailing love.

Whisper of God

Observation

Real Life Application

Daily Prayer

The Overflow of Multiplied Joy

Read Acts 8

Whisper of God

So there was much joy in that city.

Acts 8:8

Observation

In Acts 7 Steven was stoned to death because of his faith in Jesus. Saul was there as a witness and Acts 8 begins saying he approved of Steven's execution. But Saul was not satisfied. A great persecution broke out against the believers and Saul ravaged the church *"entering house to house, he dragged off men and women and committed them to prison"* (v. 3).

How did people respond? Many were scattered, but Luke does not say they fled in fear. Instead, wherever they went believers were preaching the word. Their faith in Jesus was not hidden. Instead, they preached the word proclaimed in the hope others might also come to believe in Christ as their Savior.

Philip, like Stephen, was one of the deacons appointed to serve the church. (See: Acts 6:5). As a church leader, he would most likely be in Saul's crosshair to be arrested, put on trial, and executed. But Philip did not run away to conceal his faith in Jesus.

Philp went to a city in Samaria where he proclaimed Christ with signs and wonders—"for unclean spirits, crying out with a loud voice, came out of many who had them, and many who were paralyzed or lame were healed" (v.7). Because Philp was not silenced by Stephen's death, so "there was much joy in that city."

Real Life Application

The tragic stoning to death of Stephen did not have the effect Saul and others hope for. The believers were not overcome with sorrow, nor cowering in fear. The word of God spread, so more people came to faith in Jesus as the risen LORD. The joy of these believer's salvation was greater than their sorrow or fear caused by the persecution of Saul and others who opposed them.

God's ways are NOT our ways. I would rather have people like me, but the LORD may allow adversity and persecution to awaken the Church from its slumber. We need to go into the marketplace and workplace to share our faith with those who are lost and not wait for them to come into one of our churches.

Like so many Christians, I'm easily distracted by things happening in our world today. News headlines can cause frustration, sorrow, and sometimes even fear. But far worse is how the constant barrage of bad news numbs our hearts, so we become apathetic and our faith impotent.

Nothing in this world will ever stop the multiplied joy "faithing" produces in the lives of believers. When we live what we believe, we receive a joyful overflow to share with others.

I need what I believe to be active within me so my joy in Christ is greater than the negative emotions the world tries to stir up in its place.

Daily Prayer

LORD Jesus, I confess my joy is incomplete. I need my faith to be strengthened within me to live joyfully. Our world is suffering from anxiety, depression, and emptiness. Too many Christians reflect the world and not You. Forgive me for having a weak and joyless faith because my focus is on the troubles of the world and not on what You have done for me. Holy Spirit, strengthen my faith to live what I believe with multiplied and overflowing joy.

Whisper of God

Observation

Real Life Application

Daily Prayer

"Faithing" Brings Radical Obedience

Read Acts 14

Whisper of God

> *They returned to Lystra and to Iconium and to Antioch, strengthening the souls of the disciples, encouraging them to continue in the faith, and saying that through many tribulations we must enter the kingdom of God.*
>
> Acts 14:21-22

Observation

On Paul and Barnabas' first missionary journey, the pendulum swung wide from acceptance and fame to rejection with the threat of death. Yet they would not turn back. Their belief in Christ was "faithing" within them to produce radical obedience.

While in Iconium both Jews and Greeks believe their message. But unbelieving Jews poisoned the minds of the Gentiles. But Paul and Barnabas did not lose faith. They remained in the city for a long time *"speaking boldly for the LORD"* (v. 3).

However, the people of Iconium were divided. Some believed and were saved, while others rejected their preaching. When the rulers of the city sided with the nonbelievers, they planned to mistreat and execute Paul and Barnabas by stoning. The missionaries heard of their plan and fled the city.

But Paul and Barnabas were not silenced. They continued to preach the gospel in the nearby cities of Lystra and Derbe.

While in Lystra many of the people accepted Paul and Barnabas, but for the wrong reasons. A man crippled from birth heard their preaching and had faith to believe Jesus could heal him. When the crowds saw him walking, they thought the gods had come to them. The word spread quickly, and the priests of Zeus prepared to offer sacrifices to them, but Paul and Barnabas tore their clothes to convince them not to do it. They said, *"We also are men, of like nature with you, and we bring you good news, that you should turn from these vain things to a living God"* (v. 15).

Things quickly went from bad to worse. Nonbelieving Jews arrived in Lystra and convinced the crowd Paul and Barnabas were false prophets. *"They stoned Paul and dragged him out of the city, supposing that he was dead"* (v. 19). But Paul got up and went back into the city with the disciples. The next day, he left with Barnabas to go to Derbe where they continued to preach the gospel making disciples of many.

You might think with their lives threatened and having been left for dead Paul would decide the time had come for them to just return home as quickly as possible. Instead, *"they returned to Lystra and to Iconium and to Antioch, strengthening the souls of the disciples, encouraging them to continue in the faith, and **saying that through many tribulations we must enter the kingdom of God.**"*

With radical obedience, Paul and Barnabas went back to the same cities where people wanted to either worship them like gods, or kill them. They understood the need to build up the faith of these believers and to appoint elders to lead the churches there they started.

Real Life Application

Paul and Barnabas understood the way of salvation would not be easy but filled with tribulation. Jesus warned His disciples, ***"If they persecuted me, they will also persecute you. If they kept my word, they will also keep yours."*** (John 15:20).

This is what we see happening in Paul and Barnabas' missionary journey. Some believed and were saved, while others rejected their message and persecuted them.

I can't help but wonder how my faith compares to that of first century believers. I need to allow "faithing" to work in me to produce the same kind of radical obedience to remain humble when people speak well of me and boldly stand for Christ regardless of what people might think.

Daily Prayer

LORD Jesus, how different the modern experience of Christianity is to that of early disciples. Holy Spirit, awaken me to my need to be prepared for the adversity to come as we look for Jesus' Second Coming. Strengthen my faith, so like Paul, I won't let my ego lead me astray through ministry success, nor will I fail to speak up to avoid opposition. Give me the radical obedience needed to follow in Your footsteps and trust the outcome to You.

Whisper of God

Observation

Real Life Application

Daily Prayer

God's Word Strengthens Our Faithful Obedience

Read Psalm 119

Whisper of God

I have gone astray like a lost sheep; seek your servant,
for I do not forget your commandments.

Psalm 119:176

Observation

Psalm 119 is not only the longest chapter in the Bible, but it shines like the brightest of stars in the constellation of the psalms. David wrote it as an acrostic poem of twenty-two stanzas, one for each letter of the Hebrew alphabet. Moving alphabetically, each stanza has eight lines in which the first word begins with the same Hebrew letter.

The theme of Psalm 119 is God's word, which David describes as the LORD'S commandments, law, instruction, precepts, righteous rules, statutes, testimonies, and more. The psalm shows more than his mastery of the Hebrew language and poetry. We view a glimpse into David's heart with a deep love and devotion for God's word. Little wonder the LORD described David as *"a man after my heart, who will do all my will"* (Acts 13:22).

David begins Psalm 119 by saying *"Blessed are those whose way is blameless, who walk in the law of the LORD"* (v. 1). He sings out how God's word is hidden within his heart so that *"I might not sin against You"* (v. 11). David looks with confident faith for the LORD'S unfailing love to come to him with *"Your salvation according to Your promise"* (v. 41). He affirms God's word to be *"a lamp to my feet and a light for my path"* (v.105). And he weeps with *"streams of tears because people do not keep Your law"* (v.136). But all those who love the LORD'S law have great peace because *"nothing can make them stumble"* (v.165).

These are only a handful of the gems David placed into the treasure chest of Psalm 119. He began with the blessing for those whose way is pure, and one hundred seventy-six verses later, he concludes with an assurance for the imperfect who turned the wrong way. David concludes his song with the words, *"I have gone astray like a lost sheep; seek your servant, for I do not forget your commandments."*

The Apostle Paul would centuries later confess to the Romans how he does not always do the good he knows he should, but instead, does the evil he knows is wrong. So too, David, the shepherd king, knows that he is a lost sheep in need of the Good Shepherd to come to his rescue to find him.

Real Life Application

Like David and Paul, I am also a lost sheep. I know the way God wants me to go. In times past, I have enjoyed the LORD'S blessing for choosing to follow Him in the way of righteousness. But like all of us, I stumble and fall. In these times of weakness, I'm thankful the LORD will not forsake me but will seek me out because I am His. However, we should not excuse sin simply because we know God will look for us. As David sang at the beginning of his song *"You have commanded your precepts to be kept diligently"* (v. 4).

Obedience is not achieved by our best efforts or willpower. Obedience to God's word is by faith, or the activity of "faithing" to live what we believe. My faith will be weak causing me to lose my way unless, like David, I have a love for God's Word. This is why I must remember that *"faith comes from hearing, and hearing through the word of Christ"* (Rom. 10:17).

I need to have a greater hunger for God's word, so my faith might be strengthened and enable me to live a blessed life of obedience.

Daily Prayer

LORD Jesus, You are the Good Shepherd and I belong to You. Forgive me. I'm thankful that when I'm a lost sheep, You will leave the 99 to come and find me. You know my desire to not turn aside from the way of righteousness that You established for me to follow. Holy Spirit, give me a hunger for more of God's word and strengthen my faith through the word. Make it the lamp for my feet and light for my path so I can clearly see the way to walk in obedience. LORD, give me steadfast faithfulness to obey Your word wholeheartedly.

Whisper of God

Observation

Real Life Application

Daily Prayer

When Things Don't Turn Out As Expected

Read Matthew 21

Whisper of God

And whatever you ask in prayer, you will receive,
if you have faith.

Matthew 21:22

Observation

What happened when Jesus cursed the fig tree in Matthew 21 helps me understand why God does not always answer our prayers as we expect.

The setting is important. The Passover was at hand, which means it was spring. For figs, springtime was the first of three annual harvests. Early figs were generally bitter and thrown away because they grew on old wood. The second and third harvests grew on the tree's new branches and were sweet to eat.

When Jesus did not find any good fruit, He cursed the fig tree. Jesus' disciples must have been surprised because everyone knew this was not the season for figs. Rather than watching the tree wither and die before their eyes, Mark's gospel tells us that Peter noticed the tree Jesus cursed had died from its roots the next day. (See Mark 11:12-25).

Peter and the disciples were paying attention. Jesus used this to teach them they could pray and see even greater things happen than the withering of the fig tree *"if you have faith."*

If we are not paying attention, we might think all we have to do is believe and not doubt because and God will answer our prayers if we have faith. We need to dig a little deeper to comprehend what it means for us to have faith.

Jesus was in His final days before the crucifixion. Matthew tells us what happened during Jesus' Passion Week, but the parallel passage in Mark 11 fills in the timing details. Jesus made His triumphal entry into Jerusalem. The next day Jesus cursed the fig tree and cleansed the Temple—an important connection not to miss. On the third day, the disciples notice the tree withered had died.

69

The cursing of the fig tree and cleansing of the temple is connected to Jeremiah's vision of figs—some were good, and some were bad. (See Jeremiah 24). The LORD described the good figs as the exiles who returned to God with all their hearts, while the bad figs represented those who continued in their rebellion.

In the Temple, Jesus found people who performed their religious duty and claimed to have faith in God. But they were bad figs, useless fruit that did not follow the LORD with all their hearts.

The disciples, on the other hand, were good figs with faith to follow Jesus and obey His word. On the night Jesus was betrayed, they were with Him in the garden. Jesus prayed while they slept. They were all scattered after His arrest, but no matter how much they might have prayed with faith that night, nothing would turn out the way they expected. But even they were confused and could not see it at that moment, God accomplished His will and Jesus was glorified.

Real Life Application

I have asked God for lots of things. I prayed with faith believing the LORD heard my prayer and would give me what I asked for. But God did not answer all of my prayers the way I wanted.

The fig tree Jesus cursed teaches me two important lessons. First, to pray and have faith means I will be fruitful and produce what is good and sweet. My faith is worthless, like bitter figs, if what I believe does not transform the way I live my life.

Second, when I pray but things don't turn out the way I expected, I need to look for how God will be glorified in and through my life according to His will.

Daily Prayer

LORD Jesus, forgive me for the days when my faith is bitter. Thank You for not cursing me but giving me resurrected faith. "Faithing" is at work to enable me to produce good fruit. Jesus, continue to develop the fruit of Your Spirit in me—to live each day so Your sweetness is evident in what I do and say. And Holy Spirit, give me wisdom in those times it seems God did not answer my prayer. When things don't turn out like I expect, strengthen my faith to know the Father always accomplishes His will so Jesus can be glorified in and through my life.

Whisper of God

Observation

Real Life Application

Daily Prayer

Firm or Faulty Faith

Read Isaiah 7

If you are not firm in faith, you will not be firm at all.

Isaiah 7:9

Observation

Ahaz was the king of Judah. The king of Syria aligned with the Pekah, the king of Israel, to lay siege against Jerusalem. Ahaz was terrified and *"the heart of his people shook as the trees of the forest shake before the wind"* (v. 2).

The LORD spoke to Isaiah and directed him to tell Ahaz and the people of Jude to not be afraid of these two *"smoldering stumps"* because their kingdoms were both about to come to an end (v. 4). In the twelfth year of Ahaz's reign, Hoshea assassinated Pekah and took his place as king in Samaria. Ahaz died four years later and did not see how Hoshea's kingship and the northern kingdom of Israel came to a tragic end after a three-year siege by the Assyrians. The LORD'S word was true—Ephraim and the northern kingdom was no more just five years after Ahaz's death.

A closer look at Ahaz's story shows how God was merciful to him. The LORD declared the ruin of the idolatrous nations that stood against him saying *"if you are not firm in the faith you will not be firm at all."* However, this was more than a declaration of judgment against Syria and Ephraim. God also called Ahaz and the people of Juda to repent of their sin.

The faith of Ahaz was faulty so that *"he did not do what was right in the eyes of the LORD his God, as his father David had done"* (2 Kings 16:2). King David, who was Ahaz's eleven times great grandfather, had a firm faith in the LORD that gave the kingdom of Judah stability. God promised David *"One of the sons of your body I will set on your throne"* (Psalm 132:11).

Unfortunately, Ahaz did not repent, and while some of the eight kings of Judah that followed him served the LORD, others continued to do evil God's sight. About one hundred-twenty years after Ahaz died Jerusalem fell and Judah was taken into exile in Babylon because of their sin. Like their brothers in the northern kingdom of Israel, their faith was faulty.

But God did not go back on His promise to David. The message spoken to Ahaz included a sign to come. The LORD said to the house of David, *"Behold, the virgin shall conceive and bear a son, and shall call his name Immanuel"* (v. 14). Jesus fulfilled God's word. Unlike the other sons of David, Jesus was firm in faith and without fault so that He rules forever as King of kings and LORD of lords.

Real Life Application

Left to myself my faulty faith is dead. But Jesus makes it possible for my faith to be resurrected. With living faith, I can stand upon a firm foundation. The work of "faithing" makes what was faulty firm. Only then can I live what I believe and be more like Jesus.

I need to allow the Holy Spirit to examine my faith and reveal any fault lines that would cause me to stumble and fall. I must not be blind to my weaknesses but rely upon the LORD to strengthen me with resurrected faith.

Daily Prayer

LORD Jesus, thank You for resurrecting my faith—You give me a firm place to stand, so I will not fall. Yet when I do, You remain faithful and full of grace to forgive and restore me. Thank You for being merciful to me. Holy Spirit, help me to see the fault lines in my faith. Give me sight to see the weakness caused by following the thinking of this world and holding on to religious tradition rather than the truth that comes by knowing You. LORD, I want to know You. Reveal Yourself to me, so I might not have a faulty faith like Ahaz but have a firm faith and a heart to obey Your Word like his father David.

Whisper of God

Observation

Real Life Application

Daily Prayer

Transformed by "The Faith of Jesus"

Read Revelation 14

Whisper of God

Here is a call for the endurance of the saints, those who keep the commandments of God and their faith in Jesus.

Revelation 14:12

Observation

John's letter to the seven churches at the end of our Bibles is relevant to the days in which we live. Some people mistakenly call it the book of Revelations. However, from chapter one to twenty-two John writes the singular *"Revelation of Jesus Christ"* (Rev. 1:1).

John's purpose is for believers to remain strong in the faith as they look for Jesus' soon return. Those who observe or hold fast to what is written in this prophecy will be blessed because *"the time is near"* and Jesus *"is coming with the clouds, and every eye will see Him"* (Rev. 1:3, 7). John's prophetic last days admonition was true for believers at the end of the first century and is even more urgent now because the days have never been "laster" than today.

John sees Jesus' Second Coming in Revelation 14, when he "looked, and behold, on Mount Zion stood the Lamb" (v. 1). He also saw "another angel flying directly overhead, **with an eternal gospel to proclaim to those who dwell on earth,** to every nation and tribe and language and people" (v. 6). This angel announced that with Christ's return the time of God's judgment had now begun. Two other angels made further announcements of God's wrath being poured out upon all who rebelled against the LORD and worshipped the beast.

We hear the message to stand firm as we wait for Jesus' return when John wrote, *"Here is a call for the endurance of the saints, those who keep the commandments of God and their faith in Jesus."* The KJV provides a more accurate translation of the Greek saying, *"they that keep the commandments of God and **the faith of Jesus**."*

"The faith of Jesus" is the **"eternal gospel"** proclaimed to all the peoples of the earth. This is the truth Jesus revealed from creation, perfectly fulfilled at His first coming, and will bring to its ultimate completion when He comes again. **"The faith of Jesus"** is the first faith or *"the faith that was once for all delivered to the saints"* Jude urges believers to contend for (Jude 1:3).

I think the difference between our faith in Jesus and ***"the faith of Jesus"*** is significant. We can't fall more in love with a doctrine, but our love for Jesus can grow deeper with each passing day. We come to know ***"the faith of Jesus"*** not by searching out an ancient creed or doctrine, but through our relationship with Jesus. The more we come to know Him, the more He makes the truth about Himself and the eternal gospel know to us.

Real Life Application

I do my best to study the scripture and use tools like books and commentaries to be able to communicate its truth to others. Even after years of preaching sermons and Bible studies, my eyes are opened to things I did not know before.

However, I must be careful that my pursuit is not simply to know doctrinal truths. These can be nothing more than dry and lifeless teachings. Instead, I need to keep my love for Jesus as my focus because He alone can take the truth of scripture and make it alive in me. I want ***"the faith of Jesus"*** to resonate within me, so the work of faith transforms me day by day to be more like Jesus.

Daily Prayer

LORD Jesus, I confess my sin of sometimes finding nuggets of truth in scripture and not allowing it to cause me to love You more. These truths are revealed so I and others might know and love You more. They are not priceless treasures to put on display for others to think more highly of us. All too often, if I don't let the Your faith revealed in the eternal gospel do its work in me, then it is useless for me to share it with others. When I do, people only hear me brag about my faith, and might think I'm elevating myself above them, which might be truer than I want to admit. Holy Spirit, help me to be transformed by ***"the faith of Jesus,"*** so I point others to know Jesus more and am not just sharing doctrinal information. LORD Jesus, what I have learned and know about You is still only a drop in the ocean of the infinite reality of who You are. Help me to know and love You more.

Whisper of God

Observation

Real Life Application

Daily Prayer

When Your Faith Fails

Read Luke 22

Whisper of God

I have prayed for you that your faith may not fail.

Luke 22:32

Observation

Many of Peter's downfalls and missteps were on display in the pages of scripture for everyone to see. His greatest failure was not told just once. All four gospels tell the story of how Peter denied Jesus.

What made Peter's denial so difficult for him was Jesus warned him saying, *"Satan demanded to have you, that he might sift you like wheat"* (v. 31) The LORD went on to tell Peter after he turned back, he should strengthen his brothers.

Peter was adamant Jesus was wrong about him. Others might fail and even betray Jesus but not him. Peter said, *"LORD, I am ready to go with you both to prison and to death"* (v. 33).

Jesus looked Peter in the eye and said, *"I tell you, Peter, the rooster will not crow this day, until you deny three times that you know me"* (v. 34). Peter would not just stumble and fall once but three times.

Peter and the other disciples went with Jesus to the Garden of Gethsemane. Jesus told them to pray they would overcome temptation. But while Jesus earnestly prayed, the disciples all went to sleep.

If any of them should have prayed, it was Peter. But Peter was overconfident and ignored both Jesus' warning and call to prayer. Rather than pray, Peter slept with the others.

Jesus returned and woke the disciples. Again, He urged them to pray that they would *"not enter into temptation"* (v. 46). But now it was too late. As Jesus spoke, Judas' plan of betrayal was played out. He greeted Jesus with a kiss, a sign for the soldiers who came with him. They seized Jesus and took Him to the high priest's house.

Peter followed at a distance. He sat down around the fire with a crowd of people, anxious to see what would happen to Jesus. Soon, a servant girl saw Peter in the firelight and then another. About an hour later a third man noticed the way Peter talked. Each one said Peter must be one of Jesus' disciples, and each time Peter denied it just like Jesus said he would. When Peter saw Jesus and realized what he said, he went away and wept bitterly.

Peter failed. Or had he? When Jesus warned Peter about what was soon to happen, the LORD told him, *"I have prayed for you that your faith may not fail."* Jesus' prayer changed everything. Although Peter's faith was weak, it did not fail. Peter was used mightily to not only encourage believers, but he also boldly proclaimed Jesus' resurrection from the dead to thousands including those who crucified the LORD.

Real Life Application

We all have our personal experience with failure, a time when success and doing our best illuded us. As Christians, we can all point to times in our lives when we failed and gave into temptation. All too often, my faith seems to fail as I once again stumble and fall into an all too familiar sin.

But Jesus prays for us, just like He prayed for Peter. Jesus *"always lives to make intercession"* for everyone who draws near to God through faith in Him (Heb. 7:25). Even when like Peter we do not pray for ourselves, Jesus is praying, and His prayer is effective. Failure does not mean we never make mistakes—failure is to give up and stop trying. Our faith might be weak, but it will not fail.

I need to stop believing the lie that I am a failure. I have gotten up and returned to Jesus. Now as He restores me I should, like Peter, strengthen others to not lose faith.

Daily Prayer

LORD Jesus, thank You for praying for me. Your prayers are effective and powerful. While my faith is sometimes weak so that I stumble and fall, like Peter, it has not failed. Your grace is so amazing. When I confess my sin, You are faithful to not only forgive me but to use me. Holy Spirit, continue to develop perseverance so I might always have an unfailing faith. And make me like Peter, so I return to You to not only proclaim Your word so others might be saved but to strengthen the faith of those who are weak.

Whisper of God

Observation

Real Life Application

Daily Prayer

Full of "It" to be Just Like Jesus

Read Acts 6

*They chose Stephen, a man full of faith
and of the Holy Spirit.*

Acts 6:5

Observation

While the church was working to meet the needs of widows and orphans, some felt like they were being overlooked and were not getting their fair share. This prompted the apostles to choose deacons to oversee the distribution of food. Their requirement was for these men to be *"full of the Spirit and of wisdom"* (v. 4).

Why would the twelve have such a high expectation? More than being a waiter to serve tables, these first deacons were an extension of the hands of both the apostles and Jesus. When Stephen, Philip, or any of the others stepped into this ministry, they stood like the apostles in the place of Jesus. Being full of the Spirit and wisdom means they understood the importance of humility because being given a position of service was to be considered great in God's kingdom. (See: Mark 9:35).

Being filled with the Spirit also gave them the wisdom to know what to do and say at the right time. So, the seven men chosen were given the responsibility to minister to the needs of the church and maintain unity and love among all the believers.

One of these new deacons was Steven, *"a man full of faith and the Holy Spirit."* Just as wisdom flows from the Spirit, the fullness of faith and the Spirit are interconnected. No one receives the Spirit apart from faith, and faith is energized by the power of the Spirit.

The fullness of faith and the Spirit produce something else in the lives of Jesus' followers. Stephen was also *"full of grace and power...doing great wonders and signs among the people"* (v. 8). Stephen was full of "it" being transformed from within making him just like Jesus.

We know this story is not make-believe because of how it ends. Stephen was so much like Jesus some of the Jewish religious leaders plotted against him. They accused him of speaking blasphemy and seized him. They arranged for false witnesses to accuse him of speaking against the holy place and God's law. These are the same things the religious leaders did to Jesus. In Acts 7 Stephen answers their charges, but their minds were set. They dragged him out of the city and executed him by stoning.

Real Life Application

The Holy Spirit continues to do the work of "faithing" within believers today. Like Stephen, the Spirit causes us to be full of "it," so we overflow with the fullness of the Spirit, wisdom, faith, grace, and power.

I need to allow God to do this work in me. The first way I will know that I am filled with the Spirit, wisdom, faith, grace, and power not because of the great things I might do. Amazing things will only happen when I'm full of "it" and accept with humility the place of a servant just like Jesus.

Daily Prayer

LORD Jesus, I'm thankful that I am saved and forgiven by faith in You. And by that same faith, You have breathed the breath of eternal life in me to fill me with Your Spirit. Forgive me for the times when I'm filled with my self-importance or think I'm too good for something. I will never be great in the kingdom of God because of the things I do. The books I write, the sermons I preach, the prayers I pray, and anything else I might do or say are meaningless if I am not first Your humble servant. Holy Spirit, make me full of "it" so I am not full of myself. When You make me full of "it," then I will become more and more like Jesus. Holy Spirit, fill me afresh and anew with an abundance of wisdom, faith, grace, and power.

Whisper of God

Observation

Real Life Application

Daily Prayer

Faith Never Stands Alone

Whisper of God

...that is, that we may be mutually encouraged by each other's faith, both yours and mine.

Romans 1:12

Observation

In Paul's letters to the churches, the greetings follow a similar pattern. Paul identifies himself as a servant or bondslave of Christ Jesus, called to be an apostle. He continued with an identification of those who wrote the letter with him. Timothy is named most often, but Sosthenes, Silvanus, and all the brothers are also identified as those with Paul.

Romans is different. When Paul writes to this church, he does not include anyone as writing with him. In contrast to his other letters, Paul begins this epistle by himself. However, Paul recognized that faith never stands alone.

He makes mention of his gratitude to God because the Romans' *"faith is proclaimed in all the world"* (v. 8). The gospel of Jesus Christ first preached by Peter, James, John and the other disciples in Jerusalem had spread throughout the world and was believed by those in Rome. This was a fulfillment of Jesus' final words to the disciples that they would be His witnesses *"to the end of the earth,"* an idiom for the Roman empire's world capital (Acts 1:8).

Most of the believers in Rome did not know Paul personally. They may have heard stories about his missionary journeys to other places, but Paul had never been to Rome. This is why Paul writes of his regular prayers for them and that God would make a way for him to visit the Church in Rome. He tells them, *"I long to see you, that I may impart to you some spiritual gift to strengthen you—that is, that we may be mutually encouraged by each other's faith, both yours and mine"* (vv. 11-12).

Paul recognized that despite a lifetime of learning and studying the scriptures, his faith still needed to be built up by other believers— even those who the world might judge as inferior. Few in Rome would have had the education or experience Paul had, yet he wanted to receive spiritual insight into their common faith in Christ from them. Not even Paul was a spiritual superstar who did not need the encouragement of other believers.

Real Life Application

I could not help but think, if anyone had faith strong enough to stand alone, it should have been Paul. Today, our culture elevates the individual, and this mindset exists within the church. Many Christians talk about their personal faith or salvation. Sadly, some people stand alone in their faith. They mistakenly think they don't need other believers in their lives.

I needed this reminder that not even Paul was confident enough in himself to believe he could stand alone in his faith. He knew the spark of "faithing" happened within the relationships believers share with each other. The faith of other believers will encourage and energize our faith to live each day more like Jesus.

Today, I don't need to focus on trying to encourage someone else. Instead, I need to look for other believers to inspire my faith so together *"we may be mutually encouraged by each other's faith."*

Daily Prayer

LORD Jesus, thank You for this timely reminder that I cannot stand alone in my faith. Our culture makes it easy for us to believe the lie that we can make it on our own with personal faith. Forgive me, for the times when my heart was not open or looking for how the faith of others will be used by You to build me up. The example of Paul helped me see anew how much I need the encouragement that other believers can provide. Holy Spirit, help me receive from others and not isolate or elevate myself in regard to others.

Whisper of God

Observation

Real Life Application

Daily Prayer

Faithless Belief that God's Promises Are Empty

Read Psalm 106

Whisper of God

*Then they despised the pleasant land,
having no faith in His promise.*

Psalm 106:24

Observation

This is most likely a Psalm of David because the first and last two verses were part of his sacred song in 1 Chronicles 16. Over twenty years had passed since the Ark was put in the care of Eleazar after the Philistines captured and returned it to Israel. David celebrated and danced before the LORD with all his might because the Ark of the Covenant was at long last being brought into Jerusalem.

While Psalm 106 begins and ends with praise, much of it is a lament and confession of sin. Israel's forefathers were disobedient and tested the LORD. They forgot how God delivered them from Egypt and destroyed Pharaoh's armies in the Red Sea. In the wilderness, they continued to grumble and complain. At Mount Sinai, they ignored the LORD's voice and the commandments He had spoken by making a golden calf to be their god.

Despite their sin, the LORD was faithful and brought them to the Promised Land. Yet again *"they despised the pleasant land, having no faith in His promise."* The people thought they would be crushed like a grasshopper by the Canaanites living in the land. Rather than believe God would fulfill His word to give them the land, they wanted to choose leaders to take them back to Egypt.

Time and again Israel turned their backs on God and willfully sinned. Yet the LORD *"remembered His covenant, and relented according to the abundance of His steadfast love"* (v. 45).

Nearly four hundred years after Joshua had the priest carry the Ark of the Covenant across the Jordan River and Israel entered the promised land, King David brought it into Jerusalem. As David sang a song to celebrate, he did not recall how the LORD led His people or the victories He had given to them. Instead, David remembered their sin and how they *"had no faith in His promise."*

Real Life Application

When things are going great, we can easily forget the love and faithfulness of the LORD. David wisely called this to mind, not be remembering Israel's past victories, but their sin. He knew that just like his forefathers, he and the nation could also turn their backs on the LORD in faithless disobedience. And so, he paused to repent and renew his faith in the steadfast love of God.

Today, I have much to celebrate and give thanks to God for. Yet, like David, this is a time for me to be mindful of how easily I can slip and fall into sin. A time of victory and celebration is a time to remember how vulnerable we are to the enemy's sneak attack that would lead us into temptation.

I must not let myself have the faithless belief that God's promises are empty. I need to pause and remember my sin with a heart of repentance and thanksgiving because when I am faithless the LORD remains ever faithful to me.

Daily Prayer

LORD Jesus, I praise You for Your grace and mercy. You have loved me from the start and Your love will never fail. Your love holds me securely, so no one and nothing can separate me from You. Thank You for forgiving me of my sins. No longer do I bear the stain of my transgressions because You have cleansed and made me blameless in Your sight.

Today, I pause to remember that I am a sinner. Not that I am overcome with guilt or carry the shame of my past, but like David, my heart still yearns for the desires of the flesh. I'm mindful of how easily those who know You forgot Your word and the power of Your love that brought them out of bondage. If I'm not careful, then I too can turn to faithless belief that Your promises are empty. LORD, I again turn to You and repent of my sin. Holy Spirit, help me to remain faithful, walk in righteousness, and to live what I believe.

Whisper of God

Observation

Daily Prayer

When Bad Things Happen to Good People

Read Habakkuk 1-3

Whisper of God

Behold, his soul is puffed up; it is not upright within him,
but the righteous shall live by faith.

Genesis 1:1

Observation

No one likes it when bad things happen to good people—even more if you are in the middle of adversity and pain. Such was the case for the prophet Habakkuk. He was brave enough to not only bring his complaint to the LORD but to also write it down.

Habakkuk lived in the days of God's judgment upon what remained of Israel. He questioned the LORD when he saw how the evil Babylonian empire was God's instrument to pour out His discipline upon the tribe of Judah. He whined saying, *"the wicked surround the righteous; so justice goes forth perverted"* (Hab. 1:4). Just like us, Habakkuk could not understand God's ways.

All of us are quick to compare ourselves with others. Habakkuk wanted to know why good people he called *"the righteous"* should suffer at the hands of terribly bad people? How easily we forget that we too are bad people.

The LORD was patient with Habakkuk and answered his bitter protest. God instructed him to "write the vision" so those who hear it can understand and obey its instruction (Hab. 2:2). However, the fulfillment of the vision would not be on Habakkuk's timetable, but *"awaits its appointed time; it hastens to the end—it will not lie. If it seems slow, wait for it; it will surely come; it will not delay"* (v.3).

The LORD then speaks directly to Habakkuk and all who would complain about things they do not understand. God said, *"Behold his soul is puffed up, it is not upright within him."* Like us, Habakkuk dared to consider himself and those like him righteous. However, our good standing is not determined by anything we can do, nor is it measured according to the evil done by others. Instead, the LORD gave this assurance, *"the righteous shall live by his faith."*

Habakkuk responded to the Lord's answer in faith. Even though he still did not fully understand, he determined to put his trust in the LORD. His hope would not be in what man might do for him, but he would instead have a steadfast hope in God alone.

He twice repeated *"in the midst of the years"* in faith that the LORD would revive his people in His time and *"in wrath remember mercy"* (Hab. 3:2). Habakkuk ended his prayer with a declaration of praise. In hardship that didn't make sense, he sang his hallelujah with these words:

Yet I will rejoice in the LORD; I will take joy in the God of my salvation. God the LORD is my strength; he makes my feet like the deer's; he makes me tread on high places. (vv. 18-19)

Real Life Application

When bad things happen to good people and I find myself in the middle of trials that don't make sense, these are the times for me to stand firm in the faith. I must remember God's perspective is not the same as mine—His judgment is without bias. I, and those I consider good people, cannot earn a right standing before God. Righteousness comes only by faith in what Jesus did for us and not by what we try to do for ourselves.

The activity of "faithing" in me will empower me to trust the LORD to work His good purpose in my life and the lives of those I love. God disciplines those He loves so we might learn to walk in righteousness just like Jesus.

Daily Prayer

LORD Jesus, forgive me when, like Habakkuk, I compare myself to others and judge myself to be good. Thank You for being patient with me when I complain about the bad things that happen in my life that don't make sense. Holy Spirit, help me to remember to always live by faith and not by what I see happening around me. Give me the insight to see how Your discipline trains me to walk in righteousness. And with the energy of "faithing" give me the wisdom to live in obedience to Your ways—even when it does not make sense. I give You praise and rejoice that Jesus is my salvation and the Holy Spirit is my strength. LORD, I trust in You!

Whisper of God

Observation

Real Life Application

Daily Prayer

"Faithing" to Bring Others Close to Jesus

Read Mark 2

Whisper of God

And when Jesus saw their faith, he said to the paralytic,
"Son, your sins are forgiven."

Mark 2:5

Observation

After going to preach and heal the sick in many of the cities around the Sea of Galilee, Jesus and His disciples returned to Capernaum. Home to Peter, Andrew, James, and John, Capernaum was their unofficial base of operations.

Before their ministry crusade, they were at Peter's house and a large crowd outside the door. Jesus taught in the Synagogue earlier that day, and His popularity among the people was growing. That evening, Jesus *"healed many who were sick with various diseases, and cast out many demons"* (Mark 1:34).

Word spread throughout Capernaum that Jesus was home, and people began to gather. Most likely, they were again at Peter's house. Soon, *"there was no more room, not even at the door"* (v. 2).

Four friends of a man who was paralyzed carried him on his bed to the house. Because of the crowd, they could not get close to Jesus. But they did not give up. As Jesus taught, they opened a hole in the roof to lower him to the floor. If this was Peter's house, I would have liked to hear how he responded to his new sunroof, but I digress.

The paralytic made quite the entrance, and everyone noticed him. When Jesus saw this man, He must have also looked up to see the four friends. But Jesus saw more than their faces because Mark said, *"Jesus saw their faith."* The paralytic had some faith because Jesus continued by addressing him saying, *"Son, your sins are forgiven."* Salvation is given to someone only by faith, and not by anything they might try to do to earn it. The paralytic believed and was saved.

However, the four friends looking down from the roof also had faith. The story seems to indicate that they are the ones who heard

101

about Jesus and went to go get their friend. The activity of "faithing" in them not only gave the paralytic man faith, but they did the work of faith to bring their friend to Jesus. The strength of their faith enabled them to persevere and not give up because of the crowd. They did not worry about what people would think but found a creative way to place the paralytic in front of Jesus.

The man received more than his faith hoped for. Jesus first met his need for salvation—the eternal spiritual need before the physical temporary need. Then to show the religious leaders that He had the authority to forgive sins, Jesus told the paralytic *"rise, pick up your bed, and go home"* (v. 11). Immediately, the man was healed.

Real Life Application

Like the paralytic's four friends, I am powerless to heal those in need, nor am I able to forgive anyone's sins so they can be saved. Only Jesus has the authority and power to do these things.

Too often, I find that the activity of my faith is limited to just prayer. Jesus is not limited by distance. He is present with those I pray for to meet their needs, but I need to do more. The activity of "faithing" in me needs to be willing to bring people close to Jesus so He can do the work to provide what is needed.

I need to not just pray *for* people, but *with* them. This not only brings their need to Jesus, but their faith will be built-up by mine. I also need to be in relationships with non-believers, so the Jesus in me can be close to them to do the work of salvation in their lives.

Daily Prayer

Lord Jesus, forgive me for the times when I tell someone that I will pray for them only to forget. Help me to remember to not just pray *for* them, but to pray *with* them at that moment. Thank You for this reminder that my faith can encourage others to believe, and that as we agree together, You will hear and answer our prayers. And Lord, forgive me for not being more intentional to bring non-believers close to You. I'm not called to convince them to believe nor to win an argument. Holy Spirit, help me to be like Jesus and be a friend of sinners. Make my faith contagious within these friendships so they too might come to have faith, and You can do the work of salvation in their lives.

Whisper of God

Observation

Real Life Application

104

Daily Prayer

Beyond Elementary Faith

Read Hebrews 6

Whisper of God

Therefore let us leave the elementary doctrine of Christ and go on to maturity, not laying again a foundation of repentance from dead works and of faith toward God...

Hebrews 6:1

Observation

We are to grow to maturity in our faith. The activity of "faithing" enables us to *"leave the elementary doctrine of Christ"* and become more like Jesus to live what we believe. The writer of Hebrews goes on to describe what these basic truths are.

The starting place is teaching that brings an individual to have *"faith toward God."* We first come to believe God exists. As we draw closer to God, we realize how much the LORD loves us. God's love compelled Him to give His only Son Jesus to die in our place.

When we come to God and trust Jesus for salvation, the elementary doctrines continue with *"instruction about washings."* We come to understand how through baptism we are buried with Christ and raised to live a new life. Next, we learn about *"the laying on of hands,"* which is teaching about prayer and faith to believe for divine healing. We are also taught about *"the resurrection from the dead and eternal judgment."* Death is not the end but brings us into God's presence in heaven free from the fear of condemnation and eternal separation from God in hell. (See verse 3).

"The elementary doctrine of Christ" was described as milk and not the meat of God's word. A believer who lives on milk *"is unskilled in the word of righteousness, since he is a child"* (Heb. 5:13). But those who go beyond elementary faith are mature and partake of solid food. This gives them the ability to discern being trained in the faith *"to distinguish good from evil"* (Heb. 5:14).

The difference between the babe in Christ and those who have grown up in the faith is a matter of obedience to God's word. Those who remain immature in the faith and do not mature through obedience are in great danger. The writer of Hebrews continued saying, ***"it is***

impossible" for those who have stepped into the light, tasted God'
goodness, and partnered with the Holy Spirit but fall away *"to restore
them again to repentance, since they are crucifying once again the Son
of God"* (Heb. 6:4-6)

The immature receives Jesus as their Savior but does not learn to
make Jesus their LORD. Jesus described these believers like the seed
that falls among the rocks. He said *"they hear the word, receive it with
joy. But these have no root; they believe for a while, and in time of
testing fall away"* (Luke 8:13).

Real Life Application

Jesus will continue to test or prove our faith, so it develops and
becomes mature. Faith for salvation is only the beginning. We need to
leave the elementary doctrines and grow up to obedience to Christ in
all areas of our lives. Human effort or willpower can never do this.
Only the work of "faithing" enables us to grow up and make Jesus our
LORD, so we obey His word. The mature live what they believe.

I need to continue to mature in my faith with an ever-burning
passion for Christ. Like a tea kettle removed from the flame, my love
for Jesus can gradually cool until I am unaware that I've become
lukewarm. Jesus said, *"If you love me, you will keep* [or obey] *my
commandments"* (John 14:15). "Faithing" brings maturity so I live in
obedience to His word, not by duty but with unfailing love for Jesus.

Daily Prayer

LORD Jesus, forgive me for allowing my love for You to cool and
unknowingly become complacent and self-righteous. You have shown
me that righteousness does not come from anything I have done or
might do, but my righteousness is by faith. Thank You for Your patient
reminder of how You brought me beyond the elementary faith of
salvation. Holy Spirit, You helped me to grow up and learn to discern
what is good and evil. Awaken me to how I have compromised and
give me the insight to see how I've justified my lukewarmness. Jesus,
let the fire of Your Spirit burn in me to refine and renew—may Your
fire both purify me of sin, and rekindle my love for You.

Whisper of God

Observation

Real Life Application

Daily Prayer

Longing for My Heavenly Home

Read 1 Peter 1

Whisper of God

So that the tested genuineness of your faith—more precious than gold that perishes though it is tested by fire—may be found to result in praise` and glory and honor at the revelation of Jesus Christ.

1 Peter 1:7

Observation

Peter wrote his first letter to the *"elect exiles"* (v. 1). No one wants to be an exile when they grow up because we all long for a place called home. However, more than being those who were exiled, Peter also identified them as the elect. God the Father chose them as His very own children, and that changes everything.

Those in exile live with the fear of those who forced them from their home and despair for what they lost. Not so for the elect exiles because by God's great mercy, they were *"born again to a living hope through the resurrection of Jesus Christ from the dead"* (v. 3). Death could not hold Jesus in the grave, and nothing will remove God's chosen from His presence nor the blessing of His provision.

The perspective of those who suffer persecution for their faith is everything. One can easily focus on their troubles and loss. However, Peter encouraged the elect exiles to not long for the earthly home they lost but to long, instead, for their home in heaven. He reminded them they have *"an inheritance that is imperishable, undefiled, and unfading"* reserved for them in heaven (v. 4). With faith, believers gain an eternal outlook, so they can rejoice even though they are *"grieved by various trials"* for a short time (v. 6).

To endure undeserved and unforeseen difficulties proves *"the tested genuineness of your faith."* Peter gives the example of gold purified through the fire. While we value gold, it is not eternal but perishes over time. Our faith is more precocious than gold. When faith perseveres through fiery trials, it is *"found to result in praise and glory and honor at the revelation of Jesus Christ."*

Peter wanted the elect exiles to not give up but to remain strong. Through faith, they had a deep love for the LORD Jesus. While they had not seen Him, they believe and could rejoice. With an eternal perspective, Peter assured them they would receive the heavenly home they longed for and obtain *the outcome of your faith, the salvation of your souls"* (v. 9).

Real Life Application

Peter's encouragement was not pie in the sky, feel-good theology. Peter wrote from the personal experiences of persecution, and he knew the fiery trial before him. Jesus told Peter how he would die following Jesus to a cross. (See: John21:18-19). History tells us Jesus' prophetic words were true when Peter chose to be crucified upside down.

Peter's encouragement to the elect exiles reminds us to check our perspective. So often, Christians today get caught up and complain about trivial matters with a focus on temporary earthly things rather than what is eternal.

While we may not endure the persecution faced by the elect exiles, God will still test the genuineness of our faith through various trials. We must change our perspective. Rather than desire earthly things, we need to long for our heavenly home. Only then will we have an overflow of inexpressible joy through hardships. This is the activity of "faithing" to prove our belief is authentic and greater than any adversity we may face.

I want to pass the test of faith, so I need to not complain or be anxious. Rather than worry about my home, possessions, or things I want, now is the time to look up by faith and long for my home in heaven.

Daily Prayer

LORD Jesus, forgive me when I grumble and obsess about earthly things. With this kind of focus, my faith will falter and never pass the tests to come. Holy Spirit, transform my way of thinking. Help me have an eternal perspective. Prepare me for times of unexpected but certain trials, so I will overflow with joy and my faith be proven genuine.

Whisper of God

Observation

Daily Prayer

"Faithing" Obedience to the Law

Read Romans 3

Whisper of God

Do we then overthrow the law by this faith? By no means!
On the contrary, we uphold the law.

Romans 3:31

Observation

No one throws away the baby with the bathwater. Today, however, far too many Christians discard the law and keep only their faith in Jesus. The only way to properly understand Paul's message about the law and faith is through this final verse of chapter three. Unfortunately, many believers already made up their minds long before reading this verse.

Paul asked an important question, *"Do we then overthrow the law by this faith?"* Overthrow means to cause to cease, put an end to, annul, or abolish.[1] Paul was emphatic saying, *"By no means!"* Rather than eliminate or do away with God's law, he went on to say through faith *"we uphold the law."* In this way, the law is made firm, it is fixed, and established, to sustain the law's authority or force.[2]

When we grasp how the law, and faith work together, we begin to better understand Paul's teaching. Faith as a noun is grounded in the law which is God's word and instruction of scripture. This is the substance of what we believe. Faith as a verb does not look to what we can do for salvation but looks to what Jesus accomplished for us. This is the activity of trusting belief or saving faith.

This is what I have come to call "faithing" at the intersection of faith as a noun and a verb that enables us to live what we believe. Our faith in Jesus does not set aside God's law. These intersect to produce "faithing" obedience to the law, making us more and more like Jesus.

Therefore, when Paul says, *"we know that whatever the law says it speaks to those who are under the law"* we don't quickly think we are not under the law but grace. Instead, we comprehend how Paul is talking about those under the consequence or penalty of the law who are without excuse because the law silences their argument, so *"the whole world may be held accountable to God"* (v.19).

113

We also begin to realize when Paul refers to the *"works of the law,"* both here in Romans 3 and Galatians, it is not the same as obedience to the law. Paul struggled to communicate the idea of what we now think of as legalism. However, in the first century, no such Greek or Hebrew word even existed, which is why we don't find "legalism" in our English Bibles. Legalism will never bring about our justification; rather, our effort to perform the law only increases our *"knowledge of sin"* (v. 20).

"Faithing" also gives us a greater appreciation for what Jesus accomplished on our behalf. The Law and the Prophets bore witness to how we receive "the righteousness of God through faith in Jesus Christ" (v. 22). We are sinners in need of a Savior. We *"are justified by His grace as a gift, through the redemption that is in Christ Jesus,"* not the result of legalism but *"received by faith"* (vv. 24-25).

Real Life Application

Rather than conclude faith replaced the law, I'm learning to rethink how the law and faith work together. "Faithing" is not something I do with legalistic effort. The Holy Spirit takes what I believe and animates it so I live a new life aligned with the truth of God's word. With thanksgiving, I need to look again at Old Testament instruction I thought was for a time past and see how the Holy Spirit will do the work of "faithing" obedience to the law in me.

Daily Prayer

LORD Jesus, forgive me for the times I have brushed aside Your law as no longer relevant for how we are to live by faith today. Your word makes it clear that faith does not abolish but upholds the law. Holy Spirit, keep me from falling into the trap of legalistic righteousness. LORD, teach me obedience to God's law that endures for all time. Thank You, Jesus, for all You did to set me free from the penalty of sin to live my life keeping God's law just like You.

---

[1] Lexicon :: Strong's G2673 – *katargeō*, Outline of Biblical Usage. https://www.blueletterbible.org/lang/lexicon/lexicon.cfm?Strongs=G2673&t=ESV

[2] Lexicon:: Strong's G22476 - *histēmi* , Outline of Bibliclal Usage. https://www.blueletterbible.org/lang/lexicon/lexicon.cfm?Strongs=G2476&t=ESV

Whisper of God

Observation

Daily Prayer

Crucified With Christ

Read Galatians 1-2

Whisper of God

I have been crucified with Christ.
It is no longer I who live, but Christ who lives in me.
And the life I now live in the flesh I live by faith in the Son of
God, who loved me and gave himself for me.

Galatians 2:20

Observation

Paul was amazed believers in the churches of Galatia were so easily persuaded to turn to *"another gospel"* by troublemakers who distorted the one true *"gospel of Christ"* (Gal. 1:6-7). These agitators convinced them their faith in Jesus was not enough to be saved. Instead, the Galatians needed to first be circumcised and become a Jew like them.

The gospel Paul preached was not *"man's gospel"* but was given by *"a revelation of Jesus Christ"* (Gal. 1:11-12). Paul was all too familiar with the misinterpretation of the scriptures taught by legalistic false teachers. He once believed the lie too. Paul *"persecuted the church of God"* wanting to destroy it (Gal 1:13). But God was gracious and revealed His son Jesus to Paul, so he might preach Christ among the Gentiles instead.

Paul and the brothers with him were all Jews by birth. While they were raised to observe God's commandments, they recognized no one can earn salvation by what they do. Paul emphasized that *"a person is not justified by works of the law but through faith in Jesus Christ,"* and again saying, *"by works of the law no one will be justified"* (Gal. 2:16). Salvation is a gift received by faith.

Since we are justified by faith, does this mean we can disobey God's law? Paul asked the Galatians a similar question. If by faith in Christ *"we too were found to be sinners, is Christ then a servant of sin?"* Paul's immediate answer, *"Certainly not!"* (Gal. 2:17). Works of the law are not the same obedience to the law.

Paul went on to illustrate this with a statement central to his argument. He began by saying, *"I have been crucified with Christ."*

By faith in Jesus, Paul put to death his effort to earn God's grace through the works of the law. As a result, he continued saying, *"it is no longer I who live but Christ who lives in me."* Because Jesus was alive in him, Paul no longer struggled to earn a right standing before God. Instead, Paul said, *"the life I now live in the flesh I live by faith in the Son of God, who loved me and gave Himself for me."*

Real Life Application

Like Paul, I am crucified with Christ and live by faith in Jesus who powerfully lives in me. The life of Jesus in me will not lead me in willful disobedience to God's law. Jesus perfectly fulfilled the law and commandments. His Spirit gives me the strength to, likewise, live with obedience to God's word.

I need to be careful not to fall into the trap of legalism and works of the law to achieve salvation. Doctrine or head knowledge is powerless to change the way I live. My heart leads the way to change and not my head. The activity of "faithing" within my heart puts my efforts to death, so Jesus can live His life through me. Rather than legalism, I live what I believe by faith.

The same is true for other believers. I cannot take the place of the Holy Spirit and try to tell others how to live. Trying to lead others with head knowledge only produces more legalism. Instead, I simply need to point their hearts to Jesus and the cross. Only as we are crucified with Jesus will His life be lived in us.

Daily Prayer

LORD Jesus, thank You for Your Spirit that lives in me, not because of anything I try to do but by faith alone. Your life in me transformed my heart. My head may never fully understand the intricacies of Your law, but little by little, You enable me to live a life of obedience. LORD, forgive me when my head tries to get ahead of my heart—this only leads to legalism and not faithful obedience. And forgive me for my judgmental attitude toward other believers I think don't measure up to my headstrong standards. Rather than pushing my works of the law, help me to simply point them to You and Your cross. Help me to rest in the assurance that just as You changed my heart, Your life in them will lead them in faithful obedience too. You know best how to direct our hearts in the path of righteousness.

Whisper of God

Observation

Real Life Application

Daily Prayer

Doing Away With the Me-First Mindset

Read Romans 12

Whisper of God

For by the grace given to me I say to everyone among you not to think of himself more highly than he ought to think, but to think with sober judgment, each according to the measure of faith that God has assigned.

Romans 12:3

Observation

Throughout the book of Romans, Paul shows us we come to God through faith and not by works. He tells us to offer ourselves completely to the LORD *"as a living sacrifice"* (v. 1). Every part of our lives is set apart as holy and accepted by God as our spiritual worship.

The way we interact with family and friends, our education, work, entertainment, vacation, and rest, these things are not secular compartments of our lives distinct from a sacred "God-box" of religion. Instead, our faith brings everything together in response to the LORD'S love and mercy as our service to God.

By faith, we are changed from the inside out and *"transformed by the renewal of your mind."* The activity of "faithing" puts a stop to our me-first pattern of thinking. This is not something we do in our strength. Instead, the Spirit enables us to examine every thought and *"discern what is the will of God, what is good and acceptable and perfect"* (v. 2).

How can we know with certainty our lives are offered to God as living sacrifices and our minds are transformed to recognize what God desires? Paul provides a resurrected faith litmus test. No one should think of himself *"more highly than he ought to think, but to think with sober judgment."* Paul encourages us to be in our right mind, so our attitude and thoughts are controlled. The Spirit helps us to be mindful of who we are in Christ and not forget each of us is a sinner in desperate need of a Savior.

Paul continued saying our attitude comes from *"the measure of faith that God has assigned."* The LORD has not provided each of us with a different degree or quantity of faith. God's word delivers a limitless supply. Instead, we evaluate everything we think, say, and do by the standard of the faith God gave to us through the gospel. Jesus is the truth and is the revelation of God that establishes our doctrine.

In this way, the activity of "faithing" does away with our me-first mindset. Rather than striving to get ahead or see what we can gain, we have a change of thinking to live what we believe and serve others just like Jesus.

Real Life Application

The world in which we live is relentless in its effort to shape our thinking and consider our wishes ahead of the needs of others. Pride is not the only way we think more highly of ourselves than we should. Insecurity also causes us to make ourselves great. We will exploit the weakness, faults, and sins of others to make ourselves look better, even if it is only in our own eyes.

I'm struck by the thought of *"sober judgment"* aligned with God-given faith. I need to allow the Holy Spirit to help me discipline my thinking. I need to be sober-minded and self-controlled, which is a fruit of the Spirit and not will-power.

Daily Prayer

LORD Jesus, forgive me for how I am sometimes quick to judge others. You have shown me that my silent verdict is not rendered to help them grow in their faith, but simply to make me feel better about myself. I confess that I, too, fall short of Your perfect will for my life yet consider my errors as less than those of others. Forgive me for not living up to the measure of faith and truth You gave me.

Holy Spirit, help me not be like the man who points at the speck of sawdust in the eyes of others but remains oblivious to the plank in my own eye. Thank You for giving me sight to properly see myself. Transform my thinking, so I am not held captive with me-first thinking of pride and insecurity.

Whisper of God

Observation

Real Life Application

Daily Prayer

The Great Exchange

Read 2 Corinthians 5

Whisper of God

For we walk by faith, not by sight.

2 Corinthians 5:7

Observation

Paul turns his gaze toward eternity and our home in heaven. He refers to the body in which we live as a tent. Paul was a tentmaker and knew tents were only temporary dwelling places compared to a house. He said when we die and our tent is destroyed, *"we have a building from God, a house not made with hands, eternal in the heavens"* (v. 1).

For all those with faith in Christ for salvation, death brings about the great exchange. A temporary tent is exchanged for a building that endures. A weak human body of flesh and blood will be traded in for a new and eternal house made by God. Every day we live in our earthly tent, we inwardly cry with a *"longing to put on our heavenly dwelling"* (v. 2).

Paul said this intense desire grows out of an awareness that we would *"not be found naked"* (v. 3). While living in our human body, our flesh is weakened by sin that leads to death. Therefore, we do not want to remain unclothed and exposed, but groan to *"be clothed, so that what is mortal may be swallowed up by life"* (v. 4).

One might think this all sounds too good to be true. However, Paul reminds us that God prepares all who believe for this great exchange. Even more, Jesus gave *"us the Spirit as a guarantee"* (v. 5). The LORD will make good on His promise to give us eternal life through our faith in Jesus—what we hope for when this life ends is certain because the Holy Spirit dwells within us.

The longing for which we groan is not natural. People don't sit around and imagine how good life will be after they die. Death is a mystery; an unknown people try to ignore it because they are afraid to die. Their goal is to get as much out of life as they can because as the saying goes, "The one with the most toys wins."

Not so for the believer. The Spirit replaces fear with the hopeful longing for what lies beyond the grave. That's the guarantee of better things to come. An inner confidence that is stronger than the fear of death changes the way believers live their lives. This hope is why Paul says, *"We walk by faith, not by sight."*

Real Life Application

"Walk" is a metaphor for how we live. Paul also used the image of running in a race encouraging us to *"run that you may obtain"* the prize in heaven (1 Cor. 9:24). Wherever an individual walks or runs, they must pay attention to the path before them. When our focus is on something else, we are in danger of an unexpected misstep and painful fall.

Our walk is different. As believers, we don't walk by sight. The path before us is not determined by what we can see, so we don't yearn for more of the temporary pleasures of this world. Instead, our path is determined by what we cannot see. *"We walk by faith"* with a yearning for the great exchange.

While I don't struggle with a fear of death, I do spend too much time worrying about temporary things. Anxiety is the result of living by sight and not by faith. When anxiety fills my thoughts, I need to allow the Spirit to remind me of the guarantee of better things to come in the great exchange.

Daily Prayer

LORD Jesus, thank You for Your victory over death! You died in my place and rose again so I might also have eternal life. You gave me Your Spirit as a guarantee that while my body may die, I can look forward to the great exchange. My mortal body will be changed, I will be like You and live forever in Your presence.

Forgive me, LORD, that my focus is too often on temporary things. I find myself concerned about stuff that has no eternal value. Like my earthly tent, these things will pass away. Holy Spirit, use this inner cry of my heart to remind me the best is yet to come. Help me groan instead for the great exchange. My body of sin will be done away with and I will put on my heavenly dwelling to live with You forever.

Whisper of God

Observation

Real Life Application

Daily Prayer

The Pedigree of Works

Read Philippians 3

Whisper of God

*[I want to] be found in [Jesus], not having a
righteousness of my own that comes from the law,
but that which comes through faith in Christ,
the righteousness from God that depends on faith.*

Genesis 1:1

Observation

Paul encourages the Philippians to *"rejoice in the LORD"* (v. 1). Their joy will overflow with a reminder of things he previously wrote about because it will be a safeguard for them.

He warns them about false teachers he calls *"dogs…evildoers… who mutilate the flesh"* teaching that Gentile believers must be circumcised to be saved (v. 2). We can *"rejoice in the LORD"* because *"we are the circumcision, who worship by the Spirit of God and glory in Christ Jesus and put no confidence in the flesh"* (v. 3). This is a reference to the circumcision of the heart done *"by the Spirit"* and not through the observance of the law (Rom. 2:29; see also Deut. 30:6).

Paul then goes on to do a little boasting. Compared to those *"dogs,"* he is a certified purebred. Paul had good reason to put confidence in the flesh—*"circumcised on the eighth day, of the people of Israel, of the tribe of Benjamin, a Hebrew of Hebrews."* An impressive pedigree, but Paul didn't stop there—*"as to the law, a Pharisee; as to zeal, a persecutor of the church; as to righteousness under the law, blameless"* (v. 5). According to the standards of the flesh, Paul was faultless in every way.

However, Paul put no confidence in these things. Whatever he might gain in the eyes of others with his bragging, Paul *"counted as loss for the sake of Christ"* (v. 7). Knowing Jesus was of far greater value to Paul than all these things combined and concluded that *"for His sake I have suffered the loss of all things and count them as rubbish, in order that I may gain Christ"* (v. 8). All of Paul's noble credentials were worthless garbage.

Paul wanted to be found in Jesus. He could not obtain Christ through righteousness *"that comes from the law."* Instead, Paul reminded the Philippians our reason to rejoice *"comes through faith in Christ—the righteousness from God that depends on faith"* (v. 9).

Real Life Application

Today, our joy can overflow. We don't have to do build up a resume filled with impressive credentials to earn God's acceptance. We can rejoice and be glad.

Now is the time to stop our pursuit of personal achievement and rest from our works of self-righteousness. God is not impressed.

The only thing that captures the LORD's attention is childlike faith. Through our faith in Jesus, we can crawl up in our Father God's lap because the LORD loves us just the way we are.

Paul was not concerned with what other people thought of him; he just wanted to be found in Christ. Like Paul, I need to throw away my pedigree of works—my credentials are garbage. With enough effort, I might win the approval of some people, but that counts for nothing. My resume won't impress God. All I need is faith in Christ.

Daily Prayer

LORD Jesus, I rejoice and give You praise because I don't have to try to earn Your favor. You accept me just the way I am. I know You are not impressed by my pedigree of works, so Holy Spirit, help me to rest in the righteousness that comes through faith in Christ.

Forgive me, LORD, for my insecurities that cause me to try to look good in the eyes of others. I know I'm not alone in this tiresome pursuit to one-up each other. Like so many others, I evaluate people's success based upon the wrong things. I check out their credentials and then try to measure up to their achievements. All this counts for nothing.

Holy Spirit, help me to look instead at their faith, and to encourage them to be strong in faith and not works. In the end, this is how You will evaluate each of us—not according to a pedigree of works but by faith. On that day, may we hear You say, *"Well done, good and faithful servant."*

Whisper of God

Observation

Real Life Application

Daily Prayer

Exercise the Muscle of Faith in Prayer

Read Mark 9

Whisper of God

*Immediately the father of the child cried out[fn] and said,
"I believe; help my unbelief!"*

Mark 9:24

Observation

Jesus took Peter, James, and John up on a mountain where He was transfigured, and His appearance became radiant. Moses and Elijah also appeared and talked with Jesus. The three disciples were terrified, and Peter, not knowing what else to say, suggested they set up shelters for Moses and Elijah. A cloud surrounded them, and a voice spoke from the cloud saying, *"This is my beloved Son; listen to Him"* (v. 7).

As they made their way down the mountain, Jesus told them to not tell anyone about what they had seen or heard until after *"the Son of Man had risen from the dead"* (v. 9). Peter, James, and John kept everything a secret but talked with each other about what Jesus meant by rising from the dead.

When they found the other disciples in the valley below, a large crowd was arguing with them. Jesus asked what the problem was. A man stepped forward and told Jesus about his son. This man asked Jesus's disciple to help the boy because a spirit made him unable to speak and would often cause him to convulse with seizures. Unfortunately, the disciples were not able to do anything for the boy.

Jesus spoke to the crowd saying *"O faithless generation, how long am I to be with you? How long am I to bear with you? Bring him to me."* (v. 19) He described all those there, including His disciples who were asked to help the boy, as lacking faith.

The boy was brought to Jesus, and immediately the spirit threw the boy to the ground convulsing and foaming at the mouth. Jesus asked the man how long his son had been like this. The man told Jesus since birth and said, *"If you can do anything, have compassion on us and help us"* (v. 22).

Jesus replied, *"'If you can!' All things are possible for one who believes"* (v. 23). Nothing is impossible, if the faithless will only believe.

The man responded, *"I believe; help my unbelief!"* Jesus rebuked the demon and commanded it to come out. When it did, the boy looked like he was dead, but Jesus took him by the hand, and he stood up completely whole.

The disciples asked Jesus privately why they were unable to cast the demon out of the boy. Jesus said to release someone from that kind of spirit required them to exercise the muscle of faith in prayer.

Real Life Application

Jesus was merciful to the man whose faith was weak. The man's faith was built up as Jesus set His son free from the spirit that held him captive his entire life. Miracles are intended to produce greater faith for those who are in need but struggle to believe.

I wonder. What would Jesus say to us as His followers today—would Jesus call us a faithless generation as well? We see few, if any, miracles in our churches. Some who are in need might be like the man and just need to cry out for the LORD to help their unbelief. Others might be more like the disciples who were unable to help the boy.

I fear I'm more like the disciples. As a follower of Jesus, my cry cannot be for the LORD to help my unbelief. Instead, Jesus wants me to build up my faith as make a habit of prayer and fasting. I need to be more disciplined to strengthen my faith in prayer because I never know when someone will require help only Jesus can provide.

Daily Prayer

LORD Jesus, I confess there are times when I would be part of the faithless generation. This is not because I don't believe, but because my faith is too weak from not spending enough time in prayer. Forgive me for my prayerlessness. Holy Spirit, increase my desire to spend time in prayer. I don't want my faith to be impotent. Help me exercise my muscles of faith, so I am ready always to believe all things are possible. When others share their requests with me, I pray my faith is strong enough for them to receive from You exactly what they need.

Whisper of God

Observation

Real Life Application

Daily Prayer

"Faithing" Support for the LORD and His Commands

Read Psalm 89

Whisper of God

My steadfast love I will keep for him forever,
and my covenant will stand firm for him.

Psalm 89:28

Observation

Psalm 89 is a song that makes known the LORD's faithfulness to David. The psalmist sang how God's *"covenant will stand firm for him."* The alternate translation in the ESV says, *"my covenant will remain faithful forever."* I dug a little deeper to find the Hebrew word used here and was surprised by what I discovered.

The word **āman**,[1] translated here as *"stand firm"* or *"remain faithful forever,"* is the Hebrew verb for faith. In the KJV it is translated in 17 different ways including believe, assurance, faithful, sure, established, trust, verified, steadfast, continuance, father, bring up, nurse, be nursed, surely be, stand fast, fail, and trusty.

A literal interpretation of **āman** is "to support." Jewish thinking considers faith as a support to confirm, uphold, establish, make firm, or certain. This is what it means for us to act in a way that is faithful or to believe.

To understand how God acts "to support" us with faithfulness according to His power and word is not difficult. The challenge comes when we stop to think how the activity of faith or "faithing" causes us "to support" the LORD and His commandments.

The word **'āman** is used 117 times in the Old Testament. The first time in Genesis 15:6 when Abram *"believed the LORD, and He counted it to him as righteousness."* In Exodus 14:31 the people of Israel witnessed God's power over the Egyptians *"and they believed in the LORD."* And in Psalm 119:66 David said, *"I believe in Your commandments."*

With faith used as a verb, Abram and Israel "supported" the LORD, and David "supported" the commandments. This does not mean

God was weak or needed help. Nor were God's commandments uncertain.

To think of **'āman** negatively helps me understand its meaning. When someone does not have faith to believe in the LORD or His commandments, they do not support what God reveals. To not believe means you don't uphold or obey, and you remain unchanged.

Real Life Application

To have faith and believe means much more than to know God exists or have confidence God will do what He says in His word. To believe with faith means you act with certainty and firmness to live in obedience to God.[1] The activity of "faithing" transforms us from the inside out to support the LORD and His commandments.

I need to solidify my faith to support what God says to me. Rather than justify my actions, I respond need to respond to the conviction of the Holy Spirit with repentance.

Daily Prayer

LORD Jesus, thank You for giving us Your Spirit to be our teacher and lead us in truth. I'm grateful You are helping me understand how faith functions as a verb. "Faithing" transforms how I live to support and uphold what I believe with obedience.

Forgive me when I do not respond to the conviction of the Holy Spirit in my life. Sin hardens my heart when I justify how I live in comparison to other people. This is unstable and does not support what I say I believe. Soften my heart to respond with repentance, so I uphold Your word through obedience. Help me to be like Abram and David. Neither of them was perfect. Abram believed and was declared righteous, and David was known as a man after God's own heart. Make me like them to respond to Your revelation with faithful support.

---

[1] Lexicon :: Strong's H539 - **'āman**. https://www.blueletterbible.org/lang/lexicon/lexicon.cfm?Strongs=H539&t=ESV

[2] Benner, Jeff A. *Ancient Hebrew Dictionary*. College Station, TX: Virtualbookworm.com Publishing Inc. 2009. p. 74.

Whisper of God

Observation

Real Life Application

Daily Prayer

Respond to the Impulse of Faith with Singular Focus

Read Matthew 14

Whisper of God

*Jesus immediately reached out his hand
and took hold of him, saying to him,
"O you of little faith, why did you doubt?"*

Matthew 14:31

Observation

Peter is one of my heroes. He was an ordinary fisherman Jesus called, *"Follow me, and I will make you fishers of men"* (Matt. 4:19). Peter's faith grew because he spent time with Jesus.

We all know about Peter's missteps. He was impulsive, so he sometimes said and did things without thinking. But Jesus never told Peter, "You're not going to make it as my disciple." Rather than send Peter away as a failure, Jesus instructed him in the faith. Peter learned to respond to the impulses within his heart and act in faith through the mistakes he made.

This story is one of those times. None of the other disciples were willing to act in faith when they saw Jesus. Peter was the only one to get out of the boat and walk on the water towards the LORD. What brought Peter to the place where he was willing to step out of the boat and walk by faith to Jesus?

The previous morning, Jesus, Peter, and the rest of the disciples were in Capernaum on the northern shore of the Sea of Galilee. Jesus wanted time to be alone and grieve for John the Baptist, who was executed by Herod. They all got into a boat and left for a desolate place. This, too, was a faith lesson for Peter and the other disciples. Faith perseveres through times of sorrow.

What was supposed to be a day by themselves ended up a full day of ministry. That evening the disciples fed five thousand men and their families from the two fish and five loaves Jesus blessed.

Jesus told the disciples to get in the boat and go ahead of Him *"to the other side"* (v. 22). What should have been a short journey, ended up being an ordeal that lasted late into the night. Because *"the wind was against them,"* the disciples were only about a half-mile from shore (v. 24). Jesus spent several hours alone on the mountain to pray until about 3:00 in the morning, when He walked on the water to the boat. The disciples were terrified, but Jesus told them to not be afraid.

That's when Peter responded to an impulse of faith and asked to come to Him on the water. When Jesus said *"Come,"* Peter looked to Jesus, stepped out of the boat, and walked on the water. (v. 29). When Peter saw the wind and the waves, he began to sink, but he cried out to the LORD for help. *"Jesus immediately reached out His hand and took hold of him, saying to him, 'O you of little faith, why did you doubt?'"* The two walked to the boat and got in with the disciples, who were in

Real Life Application

Rather than lose focus and take his eyes off Jesus, I think Peter was tired. They intended to spend the day alone with Jesus but were met by a crowd and a full day of ministry. While they should have made the short journey to Bethsaida about 4 miles to the northeast, they struggled against the waves for over eight hours. When they brought the boat ashore again with Jesus, they were in Gennesaret, about 2 miles in the opposite direction. (See: Mark 6:45, 53).

Peter not only learned to respond to the impulses of faith but even through unexpected difficulties, he kept his focus on Jesus. When he began to sink, Peter did not try to swim back to the boat or save himself. Peter immediately called out for the LORD to save him.

I need to respond to the impulse of "faithing" and take action with a singular focus on Jesus, who is always there to help me through the storms of life when I'm tired.

Daily Prayer

LORD Jesus, thank You that failure is not final. Like Peter, You are teaching me how to actively respond to the impulse of faith with a singular focus on You. Holy Spirit, help me to not be afraid to take the first step of faith where Jesus calls me. I'm grateful to know You are with me wherever You lead, even in the storms of life. Keep me focused, so my trust is in You, and I don't try to solve problems with my strength or wisdom.

Whisper of God

Observation

Real Life Application

Daily Prayer

Faith – A Shield of the LORD's Favor

Read Psalm 5

Whisper of God

For you bless the righteous, O LORD;
you cover him with favor as with a shield.

Psalm 5:12

Observation

David learned from an early age to trust in the LORD. As a shepherd, he watched over his father's sheep. When the flock was threatened by a lion or a bear, David rose up and killed them. The 23rd Psalm shows us how David learned to trust God as His Shepherd to protect and provide for him.

When all the warriors of Israel were overcome with fear, David stood before Goliath with confidence in God. With his faith in the LORD, David killed the giant Philistine warrior with only a sling and a stone. But Goliath was not the only enemy David would face.

King Saul wanted to kill David. When he was the king of Israel, nations fought against David. And from within David's household, conspiracies brought betrayal, exile, and the threat of death. Yet through all these difficulties, David continued to trust the LORD.

Psalm 5 is one of David's prayers, and a song to express his faith in God to protect him from his enemies. David began this song with an acknowledgment of how God would listen to his words. As a king, David knew his subjects could not just barge into the throne room. When the people of Israel had a complaint, they had to be permitted to stand in his presence to present their case.

Therefore, David did not take for granted the ability to call upon the LORD. Four of the twelve verses express David's desire for his prayer to be heard by God. He sang out *"Give attention to the sound of my cry, my King and my God, for to you do I pray"* (v. 2). Again, David sang of the LORD's steadfast love that made it possible for him to enter God's house. David sang how he came on bended knee bowing down *"in fear of You"* (v. 7).

David knows God does not delight in wickedness, nor will evil dwell in God's presence. The LORD destroys those who do not speak the truth and despises those with murderous deceitful plans. With an awareness that the boastful will not stand, David makes his request. He asked the LORD to lead him in righteousness.

The psalm ends urging those who take refuge in God to rejoice and sing for joy because His protection is spread over them. People will sing out their praises because *"You bless the righteous, O LORD; You cover him with favor as a shield."* God's grace provides those who trust in Him with protection from every attack against them.

Real Life Application

As a king, David showed his appreciation that the LORD listened to his prayer. I need this reminder. While we can come to Jesus boldly in prayer, we should not have an attitude of entitlement, nor be unaware of God's holiness. (See Heb. 4:16). I need to pause with thanksgiving and the fear of the LORD to come into God's presence.

David was also a warrior familiar with the ways of war. He knew how a shield protected him in the time of battle. I could not help but think of Paul's encouragement to *"take up the shield of faith"* in all circumstances (Eph. 6:16). Faith makes us righteous and empowers us to walk a straight path. And like a shield, faith covers us with the LORD'S favor to withstand every attack. I must have the shield of faith with me daily, so I am covered with God's grace.

Daily Prayer

LORD Jesus, I'm grateful for Your grace that gives me access to enter boldly before the throne in prayer. Forgive me when I come to You with American entitlement thoughtlessly unaware of Your majesty. Help me remember to enter Your presence with praise and thanksgiving for Your grace that opens the door. You listen to my prayer, not because You must, but because You love me.

Thank You, Father, for Your favor that shelters me like a shield. Strengthen my faith, so I am not afraid. Forgive me when I give anxious thoughts a place in my imagination. Rather than give them a place in my thoughts, cause my faith to be continual protection for my mind. I pray I will also carry the shield of faith to safeguard me from falling into temptation. Holy Spirit, lead me on Your straight path to walk with You in righteousness.

Whisper of God

Observation

Real Life Application

148

Daily Prayer

A Valid Testimony of Faith

Read Revelation 12

Whisper of God

And they have conquered him by the blood of the Lamb
and by the word of their testimony, for they loved not their
lives even unto death.

Revelation 12:11

Observation

In a vision, John saw a war in heaven. Michael fought with his angels against the dragon, identified as Satan, and his angels. Michael was victorious and cast down the devil with his angels from heaven.

The context of John's vision suggests this war took place during the time from Jesus' birth, death, and resurrection. He described a woman giving birth to a son. Her child was caught up to God in heaven before the dragon could devour him. The child is ordained to rule all the nations of the world with an iron rod and pictures the absolute authority given to Jesus. (See: Matt. 28:18).

John heard a loud voice proclaim the salvation, power, kingdom, and authority of Christ has come because, *"the accuser of our brothers has been thrown down, who accuses them day and night before our God"* (v. 10). This announcement does not refer to the time of Christ's Second Coming when Satan will be cast into hell. Rather, our accuser and *"deceiver of the whole world"* was thrown down to the earth (v. 9). John gives a solemn warning to those living on the earth to beware *"for the devil has come down to you in great wrath, because he knows that his time is short"* (v. 12).

While we have a real enemy who hates us, we need not live in fear. John shared how believers can overcome the attacks of the devil and his demons. Believers *"conquered him by the blood of the Lamb and by the word of their testimony, for they loved not their lives even unto death."* Our focus is often on the first half of what John said.

Jesus, the Lamb of God, won the war by His death on the cross. On our own, we are powerless against the enemy, but the power of Jesus' blood always defeats the devil. Because we believe Jesus died, was buried, and was raised to life eternal Satan has no power over us.

Our testimony of faith in what Christ accomplished for us gives us the overwhelming victory.

We don't often think about the second half. John goes on to share how the blood of the Lamb is effective in our lives, and our testimony is valid. He said these things provide believers victory over the devil because *"they loved not their lives even unto death."*

First century Christians endured persecution, and many died for their faith in Christ. Their testimony was valid, and they overcame the enemy because Jesus said, *"whoever wants to save their life will lose it, but whoever loses their life for me will find it"* (Matt. 16:25).

Real Life Application

By my testimony of faith, I made Jesus my LORD and Savior. My confidence is not in what I can do but is in His blood. But do I have a valid testimony of faith?

We do not experience the persecution faced by other Christians, but we do face the temptation to *"save our lives."* We enjoy comfort, so we avoid pain of any kind. As Americans, Christianity is viewed by some as being a right-wing political conservative. This causes some people to hide their faith because they are afraid of what other people might think of them—they don't want to be labeled. We also have so much that offers us pleasure, activities that are sometimes chosen over our faith in Christ.

I need to make my testimony valid by not loving my life, even unto death. If I fear what people think of me, I will never stand for Jesus in times of real persecution. If I am more concerned with the pleasures of this world, I have not given myself completely to Christ. Only the activity of "faithing" will validate my testimony of faith.

Daily Prayer

LORD Jesus, I praise You for the victory that is mine through what You did for me. Thank You for shedding Your blood for me. Forgive me for the ways I try to save my life and invalidate my testimony because I'm fearful of what people think or desire worldly pleasure more than You. Holy Spirit, give me a willingness to lose my life and desire Jesus more than anything. Help walk in obedience to live what I believe, so I do not invalidate my testimony.

Whisper of God

Observation

Real Life Application

Daily Prayer

The Faithful Blessing of Generosity

Read 2 Corinthians 9

Whisper of God

He who supplies seed to the sower and bread for food will supply and multiply your seed for sowing and increase the harvest of your righteousness.

2 Corinthians 9:10

Observation

For those with eyes to see, this chapter is a summary of Paul's teaching about biblical stewardship and giving. He concludes with an overflow of thanksgiving for God's *"inexpressible gift"* (v. 15). The LORD alone makes generous giving possible because only concerning God was the Greek word for "gift" used.[1]

Our giving is not a gift but a blessing, a statement of our faith in God. Every place else in this chapter where the English word "gift" is used comes from the Greek word for blessing and is an exclamation of praise to God for His provision.

Paul encouraged the Corinthians to prepare their gift/blessing because others will *"glorify God because of your submission that comes from your confession of the gospel of Christ"* (v. 13). Only by our faith in Christ is our generosity proclaimed as a blessing. This comes from our submission to God, a recognition that everything we possess is not ours but is entrusted to us by the LORD. We are only faithful stewards or managers of what belongs to Jesus.

Our faithfulness as caretakers is evident in Paul's reminder to arrange for the Corinthians' gift/blessing, so it would *"be ready as a willing gift, not as an exaction"* (v. 5). Extortion is a payment made to receive a benefit from another, in this case, to bribe the LORD. The alternate translation in the ESV makes this clear saying, "a gift expecting something in return," which accurately describes the Greek word used here, meaning of greed or covetousness.[2]

To guard against greed, Paul reminded them God's grace would abound in their lives to make them content and ready for *"every good work"* (v. 8). This again demonstrates faithful obedience to Jesus as a manager of all He freely distributes and is an expression of His righteousness that *"endures forever"* (v. 9). Therefore, Paul reminds us how Jesus *"supplies seed to the sower and bread for food will supply and multiply your seed for sowing and increase the harvest of your righteousness."*

Real Life Application

I have received the LORD'S faithful blessing of generosity and need to respond in the following ways:

- Because *"He supplies,"* I must remember I am only a steward and not the owner—everything belongs to God
- *"Seed"* is not mine to keep but is to be scattered or sown as I return the tithe to God and share offering to provide for others
- *"Bread"* is God's provision for me and my family to enjoy
- Because Jesus will *"multiply [my] seed for sowing,"* I must guard against greed and a give to get mindset—only as I am faithful with a little can God trust me with more
- Because the LORD will ultimately *"increase the harvest of [my] righteousness,"* I need to remember the greatest gains will not be financial but eternal rewards for faithful obedience

Daily Prayer

LORD Jesus, thank You for Your indescribable gifts to us. You have given us a wonderful home and so many other things to meet our needs. We are truly blessed by You! However, Your greatest gifts are not material things but are eternal. Gifts like salvation, righteousness, peace, joy and so much more are priceless.

Holy Spirit, make me a faithful caretaker and empower me to live what I believe. Help me return the tithe to You as the rightful owner and enable me to bless others with generosity. In doing so, let me, with wordless praise, make Your faithful provision known. LORD, You cannot be bribed, so guard my heart against greed and a hidden motive to give to get. Don't let the love for money enslave me because it will only cause all kinds of evil to grow in my heart. Instead, let contentment fill my heart with the blessing of even greater wealth, an eternal harvest of righteousness to live and give more and more like You.

---

[1] Lexicon :: Strong's G2129 – *eulogia*. https://www.blueletterbible.org/lang/lexicon/lexicon.cfm?strongs=G2129&t=ESV

[2] Lexicon :: Strong's G4124 – *pleonexia*. https://www.blueletterbible.org/lang/lexicon/lexicon.cfm?Strongs=G4124&t=ESV

Whisper of God

Observation

Real Life Application

Daily Prayer

My Life Belongs to Jesus

Read Titus 1

Whisper of God

*Paul, a servant of God and an apostle of Jesus Christ,
for the sake of the faith of God's elect and their knowledge
of the truth, which accords with godliness.*

Genesis 1:1

Observation

This pastoral letter opens with a statement of purpose. This is not a reason for writing to the apprentice pastor, Titus. Instead, Paul shared his singular heart's cry, the motivation for everything he did.

Paul's focus was not to make a name for himself—his motives were not selfish. He was a *"servant"* or bondslave, which meant his life was not his own to spend. Paul recognized his life belonged to Jesus, so his life could be spent however the LORD chose.

Paul gave himself to the LORD and others because he lived what he believed. Before looking at Paul's heart cry, some backstory will help us grasp what it means to, by faith, let Jesus spend your life.

Acts 20-28 tell a five-year story from Paul's life. The Holy Spirit repeatedly told Paul prison and affliction awaited him in Jerusalem. Rather than listen to the pleading of believers for him to not go there, Paul was obedient to the course Jesus established for him to follow. As a result, he was beaten, his life threatened, and arrested. Paul spent over two years in prison, six months at sea, and over two years of house arrest awaiting trial before Nero in Rome. During this time Paul wrote to Titus along with six other letters in the New Testament.

Again, Paul was a bondservant who belonged to Christ, so he did not live to satisfy his desires. Paul lived *"for the sake of the faith of God's elect."* This was his heart's cry. His ambition was for others to have faith in Jesus and be saved. Because he was unafraid to let Jesus spend his life, Paul shared the gospel with countless people in those five years of hardship including Roman soldiers, two governors, a king, and eventually Caesar Nero.

By contending for the faith of others, Paul instructed people in the *"knowledge of the truth, which accords with godliness."* If Paul had not surrendered his life to Jesus, untold numbers of people would continue to be deceived and disobedient to God. Paul abandoned his life for the faith so others could live with *"the hope of eternal life"* (v. 2). This is God's timeless promise, fulfilled in Christ, a message of faith entrusted to Paul *"by the command of God our Savior"* (v. 3).

Real Life Application

My life is not my own. Grounded in scripture, this statement is based upon my faith in Jesus. I was *"bought with a price,"* yet how often do I live contrary to what I believe (1 Cor. 6:20)?

Because Paul knew his life belonged to God, he let Jesus spend it. For five years he endured the hardship of prison "for the sake of the faith of God's elect." I become frustrated when things don't go as I want, and I get impatient if I get stuck in traffic, need to wait at the doctor's office, or countless other trivial things.

God put within my heart a singular heart's cry to *"contend for the faith"* (Jude 1:3). This is more than a personal struggle to know and live according to the truth. Like Paul, it is a struggle for others to come to faith in Jesus. My faith falls short if it is only about me and my salvation.

Jesus owns my life and can spend it as He chooses. I need to realize how even minor inconveniences are an opportunity for me to struggle for the faith of others. Rather than be annoyed, I need to look for people to talk with about Jesus and pray for the salvation of family and friends.

Daily Prayer

LORD Jesus, I pray the six words "my life is not my own" would not be empty or meaningless. Let the activity of "faithing" empower me to live these words and surrender my life to You every day. Forgive me for my petty frustration and impatience. When I feel frustrated, help me chose joy in its place so even the trials of life can be used as a testimony of Your faithfulness. When I grow impatient, remind me that my time belongs to You. Jesus, I praise You for living a surrendered life. You endured the pain of the cross with joy, so faith could live in me. Help me follow Your example because You paid the price and "my life is not my own."

Whisper of God

Observation

Real Life Application

Daily Prayer

Living Faith Journal Bible Reading Plan

The *Living Faith Journal* Bible Reading Plan is designed to help you get the most from your time reading God's WORD. It is set up to read both the Old and New Testaments simultaneously as the events in each occurred. Understand any chronology of the Bible is only an approximation, but it does help you to get a feel for how the events of the Bible took place through history. The *Living Faith Journal* plan will guide you through the Old Testament once and the New Testament twice each year. This may sound like a lot to read, but it can be done in as little as 10 to 15 minutes, reading on average 4 to 5 chapters from the Old and New Testaments each day. The plan is set up with six days of reading each week. This offers you one day a week as a Sabbath rest. You can take the day off, read a devotional of your choice, or if needed you can catch up on days you may have missed.

Ask the Holy Spirit to speak to you as you read. Don't make your reading just another item on your "to do list." It's more important to take time and meditate upon the scripture as the Spirit makes it come alive than to just push through the planned reading for the day.

When you finish each day's reading consider taking a few moments to journal your what the LORD is saying to you through His WORD using the W-O-R-D outline. Remember, the goal of *Living Faith Journal* is not to just hear the WORD, or read through the Bible. Our goal is to have a resurrected faith to do what the LORD says to us by His Spirit and through the scriptures. As James said, *"be doers of the WORD, and not hearers only, deceiving yourselves"* (Jm. 1:22).

January

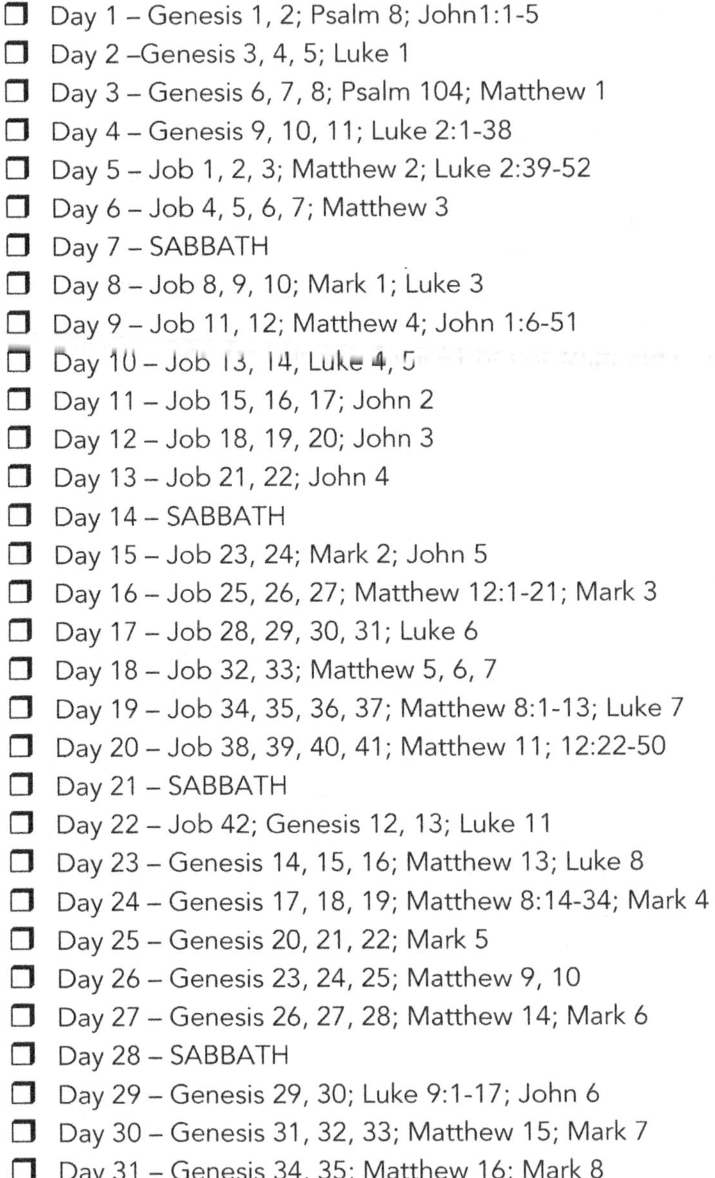

- ❑ Day 1 – Genesis 1, 2; Psalm 8; John1:1-5
- ❑ Day 2 –Genesis 3, 4, 5; Luke 1
- ❑ Day 3 – Genesis 6, 7, 8; Psalm 104; Matthew 1
- ❑ Day 4 – Genesis 9, 10, 11; Luke 2:1-38
- ❑ Day 5 – Job 1, 2, 3; Matthew 2; Luke 2:39-52
- ❑ Day 6 – Job 4, 5, 6, 7; Matthew 3
- ❑ Day 7 – SABBATH
- ❑ Day 8 – Job 8, 9, 10; Mark 1; Luke 3
- ❑ Day 9 – Job 11, 12; Matthew 4; John 1:6-51
- ❑ Day 10 – Job 13, 14; Luke 4, 5
- ❑ Day 11 – Job 15, 16, 17; John 2
- ❑ Day 12 – Job 18, 19, 20; John 3
- ❑ Day 13 – Job 21, 22; John 4
- ❑ Day 14 – SABBATH
- ❑ Day 15 – Job 23, 24; Mark 2; John 5
- ❑ Day 16 – Job 25, 26, 27; Matthew 12:1-21; Mark 3
- ❑ Day 17 – Job 28, 29, 30, 31; Luke 6
- ❑ Day 18 – Job 32, 33; Matthew 5, 6, 7
- ❑ Day 19 – Job 34, 35, 36, 37; Matthew 8:1-13; Luke 7
- ❑ Day 20 – Job 38, 39, 40, 41; Matthew 11; 12:22-50
- ❑ Day 21 – SABBATH
- ❑ Day 22 – Job 42; Genesis 12, 13; Luke 11
- ❑ Day 23 – Genesis 14, 15, 16; Matthew 13; Luke 8
- ❑ Day 24 – Genesis 17, 18, 19; Matthew 8:14-34; Mark 4
- ❑ Day 25 – Genesis 20, 21, 22; Mark 5
- ❑ Day 26 – Genesis 23, 24, 25; Matthew 9, 10
- ❑ Day 27 – Genesis 26, 27, 28; Matthew 14; Mark 6
- ❑ Day 28 – SABBATH
- ❑ Day 29 – Genesis 29, 30; Luke 9:1-17; John 6
- ❑ Day 30 – Genesis 31, 32, 33; Matthew 15; Mark 7
- ❑ Day 31 – Genesis 34, 35; Matthew 16; Mark 8

February

- ☐ Day 1 – Genesis 36, 37, 38, 39; Luke 9:18-27
- ☐ Day 2 – Genesis 40, 41; Matthew 17; Mark 9
- ☐ Day 3 – Genesis 42, 43, 44; Luke 9:28-62
- ☐ Day 4 – SABBATH
- ☐ Day 5 – Genesis 45, 46, 47; Matthew 18
- ☐ Day 6 – Genesis 48, 49, 50; John 7
- ☐ Day 7 – Exodus 1, 2, 3; John 8
- ☐ Day 8 – Exodus 4, 5, 6; John 9; 10:1-21
- ☐ Day 9 – Exodus 7, 8; Luke 10, 11; John 10:22-42
- ☐ Day 10 – Exodus 9, 10; Luke 12, 13
- ☐ Day 11 – SABBATH
- ☐ Day 12 – Exodus 11, 12, 13; Luke 14
- ☐ Day 13 – Exodus 14, 15, 16; Luke 15
- ☐ Day 14 – Exodus 17, 18; Luke 16; 17:1-10
- ☐ Day 15 – Exodus 19, 20, 21; John 11
- ☐ Day 16 – Exodus 22, 23, 24; Luke 17:11-37; Luke 18:1-14
- ☐ Day 17 – Exodus 25, 26; Matthew 19; Mark 10
- ☐ Day 18 – SABBATH
- ☐ Day 19 – Exodus 27, 28, 29; Matthew 20, 21
- ☐ Day 20 – Exodus 31, 32; Luke 18:15-43; 19
- ☐ Day 21 – Exodus 33, 34, 35; Mark 11
- ☐ Day 22 – Exodus 36, 37, 38; John 12
- ☐ Day 23 – Exodus 39, 40; Matthew 22; Mark 12
- ☐ Day 24 – Leviticus 1, 2, 3; Matthew 23
- ☐ Day 25 – SABBATH
- ☐ Day 26 – Leviticus 4, 5, 6; Mark 13
- ☐ Day 27 – Leviticus 7, 8; Luke 20, 21
- ☐ Day 28 – Leviticus 9, 10, 11; Matthew 24

March

- ☐ Day 1 – Leviticus 12, 13, 14; Matthew 25
- ☐ Day 2 – Leviticus 15, 16, 17; Matthew 26
- ☐ Day 3 – Leviticus 18, 19, 20; Luke 22
- ☐ Day 4 – SABBATH
- ☐ Day 5 – Leviticus 21, 22, 23; Mark 14
- ☐ Day 6 – Leviticus 24, 25; John 13, 14
- ☐ Day 7 – Leviticus 26, 27; John 15, 16
- ☐ Day 8 – Numbers 1, 2, 3; John 17
- ☐ Day 9 – Numbers 4, 5; Matthew 27; Mark 15
- ☐ Day 10 – Numbers 6, 7, 8; Luke 23
- ☐ Day 11 – SABBATH
- ☐ Day 12 – Numbers 9, 10; John 18, 19
- ☐ Day 13 – Numbers 11, 12, 13; Matthew 28
- ☐ Day 14 – Numbers 14, 15; Psalm 90; Mark 16
- ☐ Day 15 – Numbers 16, 17, 18; Luke 24
- ☐ Day 16 – Numbers 19, 20, 21; John 20, 21
- ☐ Day 17 – Numbers 22, 23, 24; Acts 1, 2
- ☐ Day 18 – SABBATH
- ☐ Day 19 – Numbers 25, 26, 27; Acts 3, 4
- ☐ Day 20 – Numbers 28, 29, 30; Acts 5, 6
- ☐ Day 21 – Numbers 31, 32, 33; Acts 7, 8
- ☐ Day 22 – Numbers 34, 35, 36; Acts 9, 10
- ☐ Day 23 – Deuteronomy 1, 2, 3; Acts 11, 12
- ☐ Day 24 – Deuteronomy 4, 5, 6; Acts 13, 14
- ☐ Day 25 – SABBATH
- ☐ Day 26 – Deuteronomy 7, 8, 9; James 1, 2
- ☐ Day 27 – Deuteronomy 10, 11, 12; James 3, 4
- ☐ Day 28 – Deuteronomy 13, 14, 15; James 5
- ☐ Day 29 – Deuteronomy 16, 17, 18; Acts 15
- ☐ Day 30 – Deuteronomy 19, 20, 21; Acts 16
- ☐ Day 31 – Deuteronomy 22, 23, 24; Galatians 1, 2

April

- ☐ Day 1 – SABBATH
- ☐ Day 2 – Deuteronomy 25, 26, 27; Galatians 3, 4
- ☐ Day 3 – Deuteronomy 28, 29, 30; Galatians 5, 6
- ☐ Day 4 – Deuteronomy 31, 32, 33; Acts 17; 18:1-18
- ☐ Day 5 – Deuteronomy 34; Psalm 91;
       1 Thessalonians 1, 2, 3
- ☐ Day 6 – Joshua 1, 2, 3; 1 Thessalonians 4, 5
- ☐ Day 7 – Joshua 4, 5; 2 Thessalonians 1, 2, 3
- ☐ Day 8 – SABBATH
- ☐ Day 9 – Joshua 6, 7, 8; Acts 18:19-28; Acts 19
- ☐ Day 10 – Joshua 9, 10, 11; 1 Corinthians 1
- ☐ Day 11 – Joshua 12, 13; 1 Corinthians 2, 3
- ☐ Day 12 – Joshua 14, 15, 16; 1 Corinthians 4, 5
- ☐ Day 13 – Joshua 17, 18, 19, 20; 1 Corinthians 6
- ☐ Day 14 – Joshua 21, 22, 23, 24; 1 Corinthians 7
- ☐ Day 15 – SABBATH
- ☐ Day 16 – Judges 1, 2; 1 Corinthians 8, 9, 10
- ☐ Day 17 – Judges 3, 4, 5; 1 Corinthians 11
- ☐ Day 18 – Judges 6, 7, 8; 1 Corinthians 12
- ☐ Day 19 – Judges 9, 10; 1 Corinthians 13, 14
- ☐ Day 20 – Judges 11, 12; 1 Corinthians 15, 16
- ☐ Day 21 – Judges 13, 14, 15, 16; 2 Corinthians 1
- ☐ Day 22 – SABBATH
- ☐ Day 23 – Judges 17, 18; 2 Corinthians 2, 3, 4
- ☐ Day 24 – Judges 19, 20, 21; 2 Corinthians 5, 6
- ☐ Day 25 – Ruth 1, 2, 3, 4; 2 Corinthians 7
- ☐ Day 26 – 1 Samuel 1, 2, 3; 2 Corinthians 9
- ☐ Day 27 – 1 Samuel 4, 5, 6; 2 Corinthians 10, 11
- ☐ Day 28 – 1 Samuel 7, 8, 9; 2 Corinthians 12, 13
- ☐ Day 29 – SABBATH
- ☐ Day 30 – 1 Samuel 10, 11, 12; Acts 20:1-3; Romans 1

May

☐ Day 1 – 1 Samuel 13, 14, 15; Romans 2, 3
☐ Day 2 – 1 Samuel 16, 17, 18; Romans 4, 5
☐ Day 3 – 1 Samuel 19, 20; Psalm 11, 59; Romans 6
☐ Day 4 – 1 Samuel 21, 22; Psalm 142; Romans 7, 8
☐ Day 5 – 1 Samuel 23, 24; Psalm 31; Romans 9, 10
☐ Day 6 – SABBATH
☐ Day 7 – Psalm 7, 17, 27, 39; Romans 11, 12
☐ Day 8 – Psalm 52, 56, 120; Romans 13, 14
☐ Day 9 – 1 Samuel 25, 26, 27; Romans 15, 16
☐ Day 10 – Psalm 34, 35, 54; Acts 20, 21
☐ Day 11 – Psalm 63, 140, 141; Acts 22, 23
☐ Day 12 –1 Samuel 28, 29, 30; Acts 24, 25
☐ Day 13 – SABBATH
☐ Day 14 –1 Samuel 31; Psalm 18, 121; Acts 26, 27
☐ Day 15 – Psalm 123, 124, 125; Acts 28
☐ Day 16 – Psalm 128, 129, 130; Colossians 1, 2
☐ Day 17 –2 Samuel 1, 2; Psalm 6; Colossians 3, 4
☐ Day 18 – 2 Samuel 3, 4; Psalm 8; Philemon 1
☐ Day 19 – Psalm 9, 10, 14; Ephesians 1, 2
☐ Day 20 – SABBATH
☐ Day 21 – Psalm 16, 19, 21; Ephesians 3, 4
☐ Day 22 – 1 Chronicles 1; Psalm 43, 44; Ephesians 5, 6
☐ Day 23 – 1 Chronicles 2; Psalm 45, 49; Philippians 1, 2
☐ Day 24 – 1 Chronicles 3; Psalm 73, 77; Philippians 3, 4
☐ Day 25 – 1 Chronicles 4; Psalm 78, 81; 1Timothy 1, 2
☐ Day 26 – 1 Chronicles 5; Psalm 84, 85; 1Timothy 3, 4
☐ Day 27 – SABBATH
☐ Day 28 – 1 Chronicles 6; Psalm 87, 133; 1Timothy 5, 6
☐ Day 29 – 1 Chronicles 7, 8; Psalm 88; Titus 1, 2, 3
☐ Day 30 – Psalm 92, 93, 102; 1 Peter 1, 2
☐ Day 31 – Psalm 103, 104, 106; 1 Peter 3, 4, 5

June

- ☐ Day 1 – 1 Chronicles 9; Psalm 2, 48; Hebrews 1, 2
- ☐ Day 2 – 1 Chronicles 10; Psalm 15, 22; Hebrews 3, 4
- ☐ Day 3 – SABBATH
- ☐ Day 4 – 2 Samuel 5:1-10; 1 Chron. 11-12; Hebrews 5, 6
- ☐ Day 5 – 2 Samuel 5:11-25; 6; 1 Chron. 13; Hebrews 7, 8
- ☐ Day 6 – 1 Chronicles 14, 15, 16; Hebrews 9, 10
- ☐ Day 7 – Psalm 23, 24, 47; Hebrews 11
- ☐ Day 8 – Psalm 68, 89, 96; Hebrews 12, 13
- ☐ Day 9 – Psalm 100, 101, 105; 2 Timothy 1, 2
- ☐ Day 10 – SABBATH
- ☐ Day 11 – 2 Sam. 7; 1 Chron. 17; Psalm 132; 2 Timothy 3, 4
- ☐ Day 12 – Psalm 25, 29, 33; 2 Peter 1, 2, 3
- ☐ Day 13 – 2 Samuel 8, 9; Psalm 86; Jude 1
- ☐ Day 14 – 1 Chronicles 18; Psalm 50, 53; 1 John 1, 2, 3
- ☐ Day 15 – Psalm 20, 36, 75; 1 John 4, 5
- ☐ Day 16 – 2 Sam. 10, 1 Chron. 19; Psalm 60; 2 John; 3 John
- ☐ Day 17 – SABBATH
- ☐ Day 18 – Psalm 65, 66, 67; Revelation 1, 2
- ☐ Day 19 – Psalm 5, 69, 70; Revelation 3, 4
- ☐ Day 20 – 2 Samuel 11, 12; Psalm 51; Revelation 5, 6
- ☐ Day 21 – 1 Chronicles 20; Psalm 32, 122; Revelation 7, 8
- ☐ Day 22 – 2 Samuel 13, 14, 15; Revelation 9, 10
- ☐ Day 23 – Psalm 3, 4, 12; Revelation 11, 12
- ☐ Day 24 – SABBATH
- ☐ Day 25 – Psalm 13, 28, 55; Revelation 13, 14
- ☐ Day 26 – 2 Samuel 16, 17, 18; Revelation 15, 16
- ☐ Day 27 – Psalm 26, 40, 58; Revelation 17, 18
- ☐ Day 28 – Psalm 61, 62, 64; Revelation 19, 20
- ☐ Day 29 – 2 Samuel 19, 20, 21; Revelation 21, 22
- ☐ Day 30 – Psalm 38, 41, 42; John1:1-5; Luke 1

July

- Day 1 – SABBATH
- Day 2 – 2 Samuel 22, 23; Psalm 57; Matthew 1
- Day 3 – Psalm 95, 97, 98; Luke 2:1-38
- Day 4 – 2 Sam. 24; 1 Chron. 21, 22; Matt. 2; Luke 2:39-52
- Day 5 – Psalm 108, 109, 110; Matthew 3
- Day 6 – 1 Chronicles 23, 24, 25; Mark 1; Luke 3
- Day 7 –, Psalm 99, 138, 139; Matthew 4; John 1:6-51
- Day 8 – SABBATH
- Day 9 – Psalm 143, 144, 145; Luke 4, 5
- Day 10 – 1 Chronicles 26, 27, Psalm 30; John 2
- Day 11 – 1 Chronicles. 28, 29; Psalm 131; John 3, 4
- Day 12 – Psalm 107, 111, 112; Mark 2
- Day 13 – Psalm 113, 114, 115; John 5; Matthew 12:1-21
- Day 14 – Psalm 116, 117, 118; Mark 3
- Day 15 – SABBATH
- Day 16 – 1 Kings 1, 2; Psalm 94; Luke 6
- Day 17 – Psalm 37, 71; Matthew 5, 6, 7
- Day 18 – Psalm 119; Luke 7
- Day 19 – 1 Kings 3, 4; 2 Chron. 1; Matthew 8:1-13; 11
- Day 20 – Song of Solomon 1, 2, 3, 4; Matthew 12:22-50
- Day 21 – Song of Solomon 5, 6, 7, 8; Luke 11
- Day 22 – SABBATH
- Day 23 – Proverbs 1, 2, 3; Matthew 13; Luke 8
- Day 24 – Proverbs 4, 5, 6; Matthew 8:14-34; Mark 4
- Day 25 – Proverbs 7, 8, 9; Matthew 9, 10
- Day 26 – Proverbs 10, 11; Matt. 14; Mark 6; Luke 9:1-17
- Day 27 – Proverbs 12, 13, 14; Mark 5
- Day 28 – Proverbs 15, 16, 17; John 6
- Day 29 – SABBATH
- Day 30 – Proverbs 18, 19; Matthew 15; Mark 7
- Day 31 – Proverbs 20, 21, 22; Matthew 16

August

- ☐ Day 1 – Proverbs 23, 24; Mark 8; Luke 9:18-27
- ☐ Day 2 – 1 Kings 5, 6; Psalm 72; Matthew 17
- ☐ Day 3 – 2 Chron. 2, 3; Psalm 134; Mark 9; Luke 9:28-62
- ☐ Day 4 – 1 Kings 7; Proverbs 25, 26; Matthew 18
- ☐ Day 5 – SABBATH
- ☐ Day 6 – 1 Kings 8; 2 Chronicles 4, 5; John 7
- ☐ Day 7 – 2 Chronicles 6, 7; Psalm 127; John 8, 9
- ☐ Day 8 – Psalm 146, 147, 148, 149; John 10:1-21
- ☐ Day 9 – 1 Kings 9; 2 Chron. 8; Psalm 150; Luke 10, 11
- ☐ Day 10 – Proverbs 27, 28, 29; John 10:22-42
- ☐ Day 11 – Ecclesiastes 1, 2, 3; Luke 12, 13
- ☐ Day 12 – SABBATH
- ☐ Day 13 – Ecclesiastes 4, 5, 6; Luke 14
- ☐ Day 14 – Ecclesiastes 7, 8, 9; Luke 15
- ☐ Day 15 – Ecclesiastes 10, 11, 12; Luke 16; 17:1-10
- ☐ Day 16 – 1 Kings 10, 11; 2 Chronicles 9; John 11
- ☐ Day 17 – Ps. 1; Prov. 30, 31; Luke 17:11-37; 18:1-14
- ☐ Day 18 – 1 Kings 12, 13, 14; Matthew 19; Mark 10
- ☐ Day 19 – SABBATH
- ☐ Day 20 – 2 Chronicles 10, 11, 12; Matthew 20, 21
- ☐ Day 21 – 1 Kg. 15:1-24; 2 Chron. 13, 14, 15; Lk. 18:15-43; 19
- ☐ Day 22 – 1 Kings 15:25-34; 16; 2 Chron. 16, 17; Mark 11
- ☐ Day 23 – 1 Kings 17, 18, 19; John 12
- ☐ Day 24 – 1 Kings 20, 21; Psalm 136; Matt. 22; Mark 12
- ☐ Day 25 – 1 Kings 22; 2 Chronicles 18, 19; Matthew 23
- ☐ Day 26 – SABBATH
- ☐ Day 27 – 2 Chronicles 20, 21, 22, 23; Mark 13
- ☐ Day 28 – Obadiah 1; Psalm 82, 83; Luke 20, 21
- ☐ Day 29 – 2 Kings 1, 2, 3; Matthew 24
- ☐ Day 30 – 2 Kings 4, 5, 6; Matthew 25
- ☐ Day 31 – 2 Kings 7, 8; Matthew 26; Luke 22

September

- ☐ Day 1 – 2 Kings 9, 10, 11; John 13, 14
- ☐ Day 2 – SABBATH
- ☐ Day 3 – 2 Kings 12, 13; 2 Chronicles 24; John 15
- ☐ Day 4 –2 Kings 14; 2 Chronicles 25; John 16, 17
- ☐ Day 5 – Jonah 1, 2, 3, 4; Matthew 27
- ☐ Day 6 – 2 Kings 15; 2 Chronicles 26; Mark 15; Luke 23
- ☐ Day 7 –Isaiah 1, 2; John 18, 19
- ☐ Day 8 – Isaiah 3, 4, 5; Matthew 28
- ☐ Day 9 – SABBATH
- ☐ Day 10 – Amos 1, 2, 3; Mark 16
- ☐ Day 11 – Amos 4, 5, 6; Luke 24
- ☐ Day 12 – Amos 7, 8, 9; John 20, 21
- ☐ Day 13 –Isaiah 6, 7, 8; 2 Chronicles 27; Acts 1
- ☐ Day 14 –Isaiah 9, 10, 11, 12; Acts 2
- ☐ Day 15 – Micah 1, 2, 3, 4; Acts 3
- ☐ Day 16 – SABBATH
- ☐ Day 17 – Micah 5, 6, 7; Acts 4, 5
- ☐ Day 18 – 2 Chronicles 28; 2 Kings 16, 17; Acts 6
- ☐ Day 19 – Isaiah 13, 14, 15; Acts 7, 8
- ☐ Day 20 – Isaiah 16, 17, 18; Acts 9, 10
- ☐ Day 21 – Isaiah 19, 20, 21; Acts 11,12
- ☐ Day 22 – Isaiah 22, 23, 24; Acts 13, 14
- ☐ Day 23 – SABBATH
- ☐ Day 24 – Isaiah 25, 26, 27; James 1, 2
- ☐ Day 25 – 2 Kings 18:1-8; 2 Chron. 29, 30, 31; James 3, 4
- ☐ Day 26 – Hosea 1, 2, 3, 4; James 5
- ☐ Day 27 – Hosea 5, 6, 7, 8; Acts 15
- ☐ Day 28 – Hosea 9, 10, 11; Acts 16
- ☐ Day 29 – Hosea, 12, 13, 14; Galatians 1, 2
- ☐ Day 30 – SABBATH

October

- ☐ Day 1 – Isaiah 28, 29, 30; Galatians 3, 4
- ☐ Day 2 – Isaiah 31, 32; Galatians 5, 6
- ☐ Day 3– Isaiah 33, 34, 35; Acts 17; 18:1-18
- ☐ Day 4 – 2 Kings 18:9-37; 2 Kgs. 19; Is. 36, 37; 1 Thes. 1, 2
- ☐ Day 5 – Isaiah 38, 39; Psalm 76; 1 Thessalonians 3,
- ☐ Day 6 – Isaiah 40, 41, 42; 1 Thessalonians 4, 5
- ☐ Day 7 – SABBATH
- ☐ Day 8 – Isaiah 43, 44, 45; 2 Thessalonians 1, 2, 3
- ☐ Day 9 – Isaiah 46, 47, 48; Acts 18:19-28; Acts 19
- ☐ Day 10 – Psalm 46, 80, 135; 1 Corinthians 1
- ☐ Day 11 – Isaiah 49, 50, 51; 1 Corinthians 2, 3
- ☐ Day 12 – Isaiah 52, 53, 54; 1 Corinthians 4, 5
- ☐ Day 13 – Isaiah 55, 56, 57; 1 Corinthians 6, 7
- ☐ Day 14 – SABBATH
- ☐ Day 15 – Isaiah 58, 59, 60; 1 Corinthians 8, 9
- ☐ Day 16 – Isaiah 61, 62, 63; 1 Corinthians 10
- ☐ Day 17 – Isaiah 64, 65, 66; 1 Corinthians 11, 12
- ☐ Day 18 – 2 Kings 20, 21; 2 Chron. 32, 33; 1 Cor. 13
- ☐ Day 19 – Nahum 1, 2, 3; 1 Corinthians 14, 15
- ☐ Day 20 – 2 Kings 22, 23; 2 Chron. 34, 35; 1 Cor.16
- ☐ Day 21 – SABBATH
- ☐ Day 22 – Zephaniah 1, 2, 3; 2 Corinthians 1, 2
- ☐ Day 23 – Jeremiah 1, 2, 3, 4; 2 Corinthians 3
- ☐ Day 24 – Jeremiah 5, 6, 7; 2 Corinthians 4, 5
- ☐ Day 25 – Jeremiah 8, 9, 10; 2 Corinthians 6, 7
- ☐ Day 26 – Jeremiah 11, 12, 13; 2 Corinthians 8, 9
- ☐ Day 27 – Jeremiah 14, 15, 16; 2 Corinthians 10, 11
- ☐ Day 28 – SABBATH
- ☐ Day 29 – Jeremiah 17, 18, 19; 2 Corinthians 12, 13
- ☐ Day 30 – Jeremiah 20, 21, 22; Acts 20:1-3; Romans 1
- ☐ Day 31 – Jeremiah 23, 24, 25; Romans 2, 3

November

- [ ] Day 1 – Jeremiah 26, 27, 28; Romans 4, 5
- [ ] Day 2 – Jeremiah 29, 30, 31; Romans 6, 7
- [ ] Day 3 – Jeremiah 32, 33, 34; Romans 8
- [ ] Day 4 – SABBATH
- [ ] Day 5 – Jeremiah 35, 36, 37; Romans 9, 10
- [ ] Day 6 – Jeremiah 38, 39, 40; Romans 11, 12
- [ ] Day 7 – Psalm 74, 79; Romans 13, 14
- [ ] Day 8 – 2 Kings 24, 25; 2 Chronicles 36; Romans 15, 16
- [ ] Day 9 – Habakkuk 1, 2, 3; Acts 20:4-38; 21
- [ ] Day 10 – Jeremiah 41, 42, 43; Acts 22, 23
- [ ] Day 11 – SABBATH
- [ ] Day 12 – Jeremiah 44, 45, 46; Acts 24, 25
- [ ] Day 13 – Jeremiah 47, 48, 49; Acts 26, 27
- [ ] Day 14 – Jeremiah 50, 51, 52; Acts 28
- [ ] Day 15 – Lamentations 1, 2, 3:1-36; Colossians 1, 2
- [ ] Day 16 – Lamentations 3:37-66; 4, 5; Colossians 3, 4
- [ ] Day 17 – Ezekiel 1, 2, 3; Philemon 1
- [ ] Day 18 – SABBATH
- [ ] Day 19 – Ezekiel 4, 5, 6; Ephesians 1, 2
- [ ] Day 20 – Ezekiel 7, 8, 9; Ephesians 3, 4
- [ ] Day 21 – Ezekiel 10, 11, 12; Ephesians 5, 6
- [ ] Day 22 – Ezekiel 13, 14, 15; Philippians 1, 2
- [ ] Day 23 – Ezekiel 16, 17, 18; Philippians 3, 4
- [ ] Day 24 – Ezekiel 19, 20, 21; 1 Timothy 1, 2
- [ ] Day 25 – SABBATH
- [ ] Day 26 – Ezekiel 22, 23, 24; 1 Timothy 3, 4
- [ ] Day 27 – Ezekiel 25, 26, 27; 1 Timothy 5, 6
- [ ] Day 28 – Ezekiel 28, 29, 30; Titus 1, 2, 3
- [ ] Day 29 – Ezekiel 31, 32, 33; 1 Peter 1, 2
- [ ] Day 30 – Ezekiel 34, 35, 36; 1 Peter 3, 4, 5

December

- ☐ Day 1 – Ezekiel 37, 38, 39; Hebrews 1, 2
- ☐ Day 2 – SABBATH
- ☐ Day 3 – Ezekiel 40, 41, 42; Hebrews 3, 4
- ☐ Day 4 – Ezekiel 43, 44, 45; Hebrews 5, 6
- ☐ Day 5 – Ezekiel 46, 47, 48; Hebrews 7, 8
- ☐ Day 6 – Joel 1, 2, 3; Hebrews 9, 10
- ☐ Day 7 – Daniel 1, 2, 3; Hebrews 11
- ☐ Day 8 – Daniel 4, 5, 6; Hebrews 12, 13
- ☐ Day 9 – SABBATH
- ☐ Day 10 – Daniel 7, 8, 9; 2 Timothy 1, 2
- ☐ Day 11 – Daniel 10, 11, 12; 2 Timothy 3, 4
- ☐ Day 12 – Ezra 1, 2, 3; 2 Peter 1, 2, 3
- ☐ Day 13 – Psalm 137; Ezra 4, 5, 6; Jude 1
- ☐ Day 14 –Haggai 1, 2; 1 John 1, 2, 3
- ☐ Day 15 – Zechariah 1, 2, 3; 1 John 4, 5
- ☐ Day 16 – SABBATH
- ☐ Day 17 – Zechariah 4, 5, 6; 2 John; 3 John
- ☐ Day 18 – Zechariah 7, 8, 9; Revelation 1, 2
- ☐ Day 19 – Zechariah 10, 11, 12; Revelation 3, 4
- ☐ Day 20 – Zechariah 13, 14; Revelation 5, 6
- ☐ Day 21 – Esther 1, 2, 3; Revelation 7, 8
- ☐ Day 22 – Esther 4, 5, 6; Revelation 9, 10
- ☐ Day 23 – SABBATH
- ☐ Day 24 – Esther 7, 8, 9, 10; Revelation 11
- ☐ Day 25 – Ezra 7, 8, 9, 10; Revelation 12, 13
- ☐ Day 26 – Nehemiah 1, 2, 3, 4; Revelation 14, 15
- ☐ Day 27 – Nehemiah 5, 6, 7, 8; Revelation 16
- ☐ Day 28 – Nehemiah 9, 10, 11; Revelation 17, 18
- ☐ Day 29 – Nehemiah 12, 13; Psalm 126; Revelation 19, 20
- ☐ Day 30 – SABBATH
- ☐ Day 31 – Malachi 1, 2, 3, 4; Revelation 21, 22

When something is dead within you, remove it. Otherwise, you will die.

A pandemic of dead faith threatens Christians today because, in one way or another, the various doctrines held by our churches were added to or subtracted from the faith first given by Jesus. With a singular heart's cry, D. Greg Ebie resonates Jude's ancient challenge for believers to "contend for the faith that was once for all delivered to the saints" (Jude 1:3).

Resurrected Faith will encourage you to know Jesus and follow His example by "faithing." An intersection of faith, as a noun and a verb, "faithing" will bring what you believe to life, as the power of the Holy Spirit daily transforms your thoughts, words, and actions.

In Resurrected Faith, you will discover the symptoms of dead faith and why we must contend for the faith. Our struggle is to:
- know Jesus and not a creed
- recognize the enemy within
- comprehend our identity in Christ
- defend the faith against masquerading wolves
- stand ready for judgment day
- recognize false teaching designed to lead us astray
- contend without being contentious maintain unity

Your faith will come alive through an intimate knowledge of Jesus. The Holy Spirit will bring to life the true identity of Jesus to define our doctrines, rather than lifeless church creeds to portray an inaccurate caricature of His identity. Now is the time for Resurrected Faith.

- **Doug Clay**, General Superintendent of the Assemblies of God, writes, "*Resurrected Faith* delivers a passion for the faith."
- Missionary **Steve Walent** observes, "*Resurrected Faith* ignites the life of Christ in us, which is the game-changer our world needs."

Available at https://firmfoundationtoday.com/books

GOD'S CLOCK: Jesus Within the LORD'S Appointed Times introduces us to the Jesus we never knew. God's Clock is seen in the signs and season established at creation; once set it has continued to point to Jesus and make Him known. According to the timing of God's eternal clock Jesus perfectly fulfilled and accomplished God's plan of redemption at His first coming, and He will ultimately bring the LORD'S appointed times to completion when He returns.

"These are a shadow of the things that were to come; the reality, however, is found in Christ." (Col. 2:17)

Finding Financial Freedom: Your Key to Debt Free Living helps you cut a key forged in the principles of biblical stewardship. Just as a locksmith cuts a key to open a lock, your key will have seven notches to unlock your finances and eliminate all your debts – from credit cards to your mortgage in as little as five to eight years.

Finding Financial Freedom is a workbook with blanks to fill-in, space for notes and a complete set of worksheets for you to develop your *Step Up Debt Elimination Plan*. The footnotes make it possible for you to use the book on its own. However, it was designed to be used as part of a live three part seminar. If you would like to have a **Finding Financial Freedom Seminar** at your church please contact Greg Ebie at ***greg@firmfoundationtoday.com*** for more information.

Available at https://firmfoundationtoday.com/books

Made in the USA
Monee, IL
08 July 2026

56711436R00105